The Onlooker Looks Back

by

Jim Hough

Charlen –
thank for you
loyalty to the Alaskan
you are grad
Jim Hough

Kin Press
2411 Fairfax Road
Lansing, Michigan 48910

Designed and edited by Sharon Emery

To my wife, Darl

Because of my blindness, she has daily served as my reader and my cab driver through twenty-five years of Onlooker columns. She found time to do all that while raising our two children, Linda and Steve, and while maintaining a successful career of her own as a school teacher. And now she has made this book possible by personally pawing through nearly eight thousand columns, to select those for this book. How can a man express his gratitude for the love of such a woman?

(Special thanks to two dear friends, Sharon Emery Schneider and John Schneider, of Kin Press. Without their advice and guidance, this book could not have happened.)

A FORWARD

Just what is the Onlooker column? Just what is a newspaper columnist?

I have given murky, awkward, confused answers to those questions, put to me often over my twenty-five years of column authorship. But readers easily give clear and perceptive answers to those questions. That has always amazed me. Readers know more about a column and its author than the columnist himself.

I remember, for instance, the time I was on vacation and a colleague, Mark Nixon, was asked to do a column. He began by writing, "I have nothing to say."

Mark's guest column brought a response from John Ball, an industrial and financial consultant who lives in Okemos. John said a reader's view of a columnist is different than a columnist's view of a columnist. He wrote:

"A columnist who is worth his salt has eyes that see more than ordinary eyes and ears that hear more. The little things that ordinary eyes and ears miss have special meaning for him, and he cherishes them. He thinks about them with awe, or indignation, or amazement, or love, and sharing them is a natural impulse for him.

"He finds more things to share every day than could possibly fit into thirty-six inches of typeset newsprint. His real problem is not finding something to say, but deciding what to leave out.

"Leave out the trivial? No, for the trivial is the stuff of life, the spark of poetry. His best columns — the ones that bring back stacks of letters, that bring tears to the eyes, that are clipped out carefully and pressed in the Bible, that brighten the day of the whole city — are trivia crossed with genius.

"Knowing which trivia to share — ah, there's the rub. This skill is not born but made. Show me a columnist who knows which trivia to share, and I'll show you a columnist who knows his readers — knows them as individuals, reads and cares about their letters, and simply and directly relates to them as human beings every day in his column.

"These are the things that make a columnist, whether he can make the language sing or not. But if he can write — if he can really write — you have an institution, a franchise, an Arnold Palmer of a columnist, one for his paper and readers to be proud of.

"Writing a column looks easy, real easy, like Arnie's touch with a wedge. Treat it with respect, Mark, joking or not, or Jim Hough's loyal army might just feel compelled to bypass your byline."

— **Jim Hough**

5

In Memory of a Milkman

He was the last Lansing milkman with a horse-drawn milk wagon. I knew him well.

He and his horse, Charlie, were a perfect pair — characters both. He with a great sense of humor and lengthy list of devoted customers. Charlie with some zany habits that often got them both into trouble.

Charlie loved to pull his milk wagon up behind a car waiting at a light and then lift his right front hoof high in the air and bring it down with a clunk on the trunk lid of the car. Charlie also enjoyed eating up beautiful flowers — causing his driver to get some stern lectures from homeowners.

When Charlie died of old age, that milkman wrote an obituary. It was so filled with warmth and love that the editors of the Lansing State Journal put it on the front page.

If there's a heaven, that milkman and his horse are reunited now. The milkman died Thursday.

I remember that man when he worked on the railroad for thirty-five cents an hour. Anything to provide for his family. I remember him walking home from that job — a three-mile walk. When he reached home, he'd collapse — the varicose veins bulging in his legs in large blue streaks. Railroad work was the pits in those days.

I remember the time he sold his favorite possession — a deer rifle — so he could buy a used bicycle for his son.

I remember the first time he let his son drive a car. The son missed the brake pedal and hit the accelerator. The old car crashed through a picket fence in the yard and nearly crashed into the house. The son got a driving lesson he never forgot.

Years passed. The man graduated from the railroad job to a highway maintenance and snowplowing job. Folks in the Upper Peninsula still talk about the time he made a snowplow trip at great personal risk in a howling blizzard because a school bus was missing on its run from Brimley to Strongs. The bus was buried in a huge drift about fifteen miles from its destination.

About twenty kids on that bus were filled with terror. The bus had long ago run out of gas. It was an ice box. The fear of death was strong. It showed on the face of the bus driver. It spread to the kids. It was near midnight. The end had come to those on that bus.

Suddenly, there was the sound of an engine, the flash of a light. Shoveling could be heard outside the bus door. The door opened. A man stepped inside.

"Relax," he said, "you are all safe. I have some gas for the bus and we'll soon have some heat."

I sat aboard that bus. I was a fifteen-year-old boy, a freshman at Brimley High School. Never in my life have I felt more pride than I did at that moment. The kids on the bus even patted me on the back and offered congratulations. That warm and courageous man who came to our rescue was my dad, James Hough, Sr.

Parkinson's disease is devastating. For the past few weeks, he didn't even know Myrle, his wife of fifty-three years. For me, my brother Don, and two sisters Marlene and Joyce, those visits to the nursing home were pure torture. We didn't want to remember him that way; we won't remember him that way.

Personally, I'd like to think he's taking a big bag of oats to his old horse Charlie right now.

Little Linda Is Grown

She was only about two years old when she found a seagull feather on the shore of Lake Superior. For a long time it was her most treasured possession. She liked to tickle her nose with it. She looked so cute when she wrinkled that nose and smiled at her daddy.

At night, after the campfire had died down, she would crawl up into my lap and say, "Daddy, call the whippoorwill." I'd whistle the whippoorwill's song, and soon the answer would come. One night, the whippoorwill flew in to sit on top of our tent. That still ranks as one of her biggest thrills.

The years passed. She grew to be a beautiful, charming and intelligent young woman. Paradise and our cabin had a lot to do with that.

I have other glimpses of the past. Like the time I stopped to rest after walking on snowshoes, pulling a toboggan loaded with food, clothes and two children, for the mile-long trip through the swamp from the main road to the cabin. We were heading in for our annual Christmas vacation at the cabin. I sat on the toboggan next to Linda, who was then about ten years old. I'll always remember the wrinkled nose as she smiled at me and said, "Daddy, aren't the trees pretty? They look like they have white lace."

She was not a good judge of Christmas trees. Her brother, Steve, always cut the tree, but Linda insisted on choosing it. Each year they dragged in the scraggliest old swamp balsam. I'll admit, though, that it was always a special tree after Linda decorated it.

And there were the sandcastles and the frog races on the beach. And the time she investigated a beehive and the occupants invaded her hooded sweatshirt.

And the light in her eyes when we gave her a canoe for her fourteenth birthday. And how she loved the wild flowers. (All things growing wild are so precious to Linda.) And the day I took her fishing with her brand new rod and reel. On the first cast, she threw it into the lake. She cried the rest of the day.

But, time passes. She grew up — got a degree at MSU and met an exceptionally fine young man, Robert Cornell, of Mason. Several months ago, they sat in our living room to tell my wife Darl and me that they wanted to be married in front of our Paradise cabin, on the shore of Lake Superior. It figured that she'd want to observe that very important event in that very important place.

"There is sadness about it, though," Linda said, "because Tex can't be there. Oh, how I'd love to have him there."

Sylvester "Tex" Eggert died recently. He was an oldtimer who

9

lived his life on the shore of Lake Superior and made his way as a commercial fisherman. More importantly, he had become like a grandfather to my children. Pictures of Linda and Steve were prominent on the walls of his home. How thrilled he would have been to watch that wedding ceremony.

The wedding was set for 2 p.m. Saturday. It rained, lightning flashed and thunder roared all day Friday, and the black clouds and rain remained on Saturday morning.

Linda was determined to share her wedding day with Tex, so she visited his grave. As she placed wild flowers on the grave, she said, "Boy, if Tex was here, he'd just demand that God do something about this weather today."

She left that grave, and before she reached the car, the clouds passed. The sun came out bright and clear.

As I walked her down our board sidewalk and left her there on the beach, so beautiful in the wedding gown once worn by her mother, there were many things running through my mind. One of them was: "Thank you, Tex."

My last glimpse was of my new son-in-law Bob, his father Charles Cornell, my son Steve, and Judge Charles Filice, standing there around Linda, the sun glistening off the lake. That's when the tears took over.

Later, I learned that everyone cried there that day. It was a beautiful thing. That picture will go on my wall, right next to the one in which that little girl stands on the shore of Lake Superior, tickling her nose with a seagull feather.

Newsroom Legend

When the Onlooker column became a daily feature under my byline about twenty years ago, I had little idea of what scope and tone the column should take.

That was when a great person came to my rescue. His name — Fred C. Olds. He was a State Journal copy editor. He took my copy each day and worked with me. Together, we arrived at a direction and a style.

Today, readership surveys show that this column has many, many readers. I want you to know that this is due in no small way to the sensitivity, professionalism and compassion of Fred Olds. I said for many years that the column should have carried a double byline — that of the writer and that of the great editor.

I was never able to say this until now, because Fred would not allow it. He died Thursday in Florida at age sixty-five, three years after his retirement.

There are many skilled newsroom technicians behind every well-known byline in a newspaper. They may be taken for granted by the readers, but never by the writers.

Fred's wry sense of humor and the skills he brought here for thirty-seven years were newsroom legend.

He had a quiet and yet powerful laugh. Let me explain. He liked nothing more than to see the readers get on my back about something. When he was especially amused at something, Fred would slowly build a large grin, slowly push his chair away from his desk and slowly start a laugh. It would build up. Slowly he would take off his glasses, slowly slap his knee and then break into an uproarious laugh.

How he loved trains. He was, in fact, a national expert on railroads. A history buff and a student of railroading in the lumbering days, Fred wrote articles for many magazines.

His sense of humor made him tough to beat on the golf course. He'd make his opponent laugh and thus, destroy his concentration.

This newsroom was a gloomy place for everyone the day Fred retired — not only because we'd miss him in the office, but because doctors had just diagnosed cancer in him. He knew his time was short. He even handled that with skill and grace.

I did not like Fred Olds, I loved him.

Crowning Glory

Remind me to call Dr. John Neuman one of these days. I have to do some follow-up investigative reporting and find out whatever happened to his gold crown.

Neuman, a Lansing physician, and I were together recently when I noticed he was constantly pushing his tongue around in the side of his mouth.

"What's wrong with your mouth, John?" I asked.

"Nothing," he snapped, obviously eager to be off that subject.

I pressed on, as any good reporter should, until I got the facts — some from John and some from his office staff.

It seems that he had lost a gold crown from his mouth. He had no idea where it was. He had searched his home, his office, his garden. Finally, it occurred to him that he might have swallowed it. He began calculations about how many hours it takes for material to pass in and out of a human body.

Suddenly, a brilliant medical idea struck him. He had X-rays taken of his intestines. Sure enough, there it was — about one day away from emergence.

It reminded me of the time years ago when my brother Don swallowed a penny. We had outside plumbing in those days, and my mom wanted to make sure the penny passed through. So, she made Don use a thunder mug inside the house. I remember that morning years ago, when we all heard the "plink" of that penny. Success.

I wonder if Neuman's gold crown went "plink" or "plunk," because I'm sure he used a thunder mug for a day or two. After all, there was two hundred dollars worth of gold in that crown.

I told Doc Neuman that I'd check to see if his mouth was back to normal the next time I saw him. Then I said I'd check with his dentist to see if a new gold crown had been installed. If not, we'd all know what happened to the old one, and it would make a great subject for an Onlooker column.

"I'm not worried, Jim. No writer — especially one of your diminished talent — could clean up that story enough to make supper-time reading in an afternoon daily newspaper," Neuman said.

Some Onlooker columns are harder to write than others.

A Mark of Love

It's a bit dumb to assert, as many people do, that there is a silver lining in every tragedy.

But it is easy to assert that tragedy often brings out the best in people. It has a way of opening the heart.

I will never forget the outpouring of warmth and concern shown to me by readers of this column following the death of my father. I guess one expects to hear from relatives and close friends at such a time, but the mail and phone calls I received from column readers — all strangers to me — have left an indelible mark on my life — a mark of love.

Some visited at the funeral home, some wrote letters, some called and some even attended the funeral service. I counted more than one hundred such responses from total strangers.

To be honest, I really worried about writing a column about my father. I feared it might be a selfish thing to do in this column, a thing readers might resent.

They didn't. Instead, their compassion flowed in the mail that covered my desk. Here are three typical letters from those strangers. You'll see why they touched me so.

Richard Gonzalez, of East Lansing, wrote:

"Every once in a while, one of your columns touches a sore spot, and I've been tempted to write asking, what makes Jim Hough tick?

"You answered that question for all time with your tribute to your father. Tears came streaming down my cheeks as I remembered my own father's death. You have written for all of us who never found the right words to express our emotions."

Patricia VanAntwerp, of Lansing, wrote:

"I was so sorry to read about the death of your father. My eyes were filled with tears before I had finished reading your column in Friday's paper. The tears were not only for your loss, but for the loss of my father and grandfather, whom I miss very much.

"I was again reminded of how we take so much of our lives, and those of our loved ones, for granted.

"At this holiday season, may we all be thankful for what we have and for those near and dear to us. Thank you, Jim, for reminding us of what Christmas really means.

"My sympathy extends to your entire family."

Dorothy Prawat, of Williamston, wrote:

"Thank you for your very touching article about your dad. I started

13

to skim it and then had to read the entire article. It was so beautiful that I cried.

"I'm sorry that your dad has suffered, and that you and your family must have heavy hearts at this time, but your article must surely mean a lot to the people who have read it.

"I cried not because your dad has died, but because he was a simple, good man. At this time, with pressures to buy the right gift and get the right amount of toys for children, so they won't be disappointed on Christmas morning — but knowing that they don't need even one more thing — your article was especially meaningful.

"It reminded me of the values that we are supposed to hold so dear, but too often lose sight of."

See what I mean? Onlooker readers are a special breed. In your unique way, you lifted me above tragedy. You even made a Merry Christmas possible. My writing skills are not adequate to express my thanks.

Setting Sights High

If I could only write a newspaper story in braille.

There is so much I'd like to say to the twenty-seven courageous young men and women who received their diplomas Wednesday night from the Michigan School for the Blind.

I'd like to write in braille about the beaming faces of proud parents that I saw behind the cameras and popping flashbulbs, as the school's dedicated superintendent, Dr. Robert Thompson, presented the diplomas.

I'd like to write in braille about the processional and tell how those blind seniors marched flawlessly down the aisle and up the stairs to the stage — the girls in beautiful white gowns, the boys in blue.

I'd like to write in braille about how I heard a man say, "Just look at that line of beautiful kids. There's not a Hippie in the bunch."

Blind students don't have time to be Hippies, they are too busy meeting the world's challenges. And the way they meet those challenges is an inspiration.

A beautiful commencement procession, with the emotional sound of "Pomp and Circumstance," is always impressive, but try watching a procession of blind students. Wow! That will put a lump in any throat.

I'd like to write a special story about one of the blind graduates, Stevie Wonder. I'd like to tell how proud folks were of the nineteen-year-old musician who gained international fame during the seven years he was enrolled at the school. When Dr. Thompson handed Stevie that diploma, the lad's smile was the broadest in the Midwest, and you should have seen the tight grip he put on that diploma.

If I could write in braille, I'd tell Stevie that I never heard an audience jump up with such booming applause as it did when he received a succession of awards last night. Surely, the roof of the Lions Hall Auditorium raised up about three inches with that applause. Stevie's record hits, which have sold millions ("For Once in My Life" and "Fingertips"), never received greater applause.

But, if I could write in braille, I'd also tell Stevie how his harmonica recording of "Alphie" just...well, it just brings out the goose bumps on me. Wow! What a young man he is.

Many honors and citations were handed Stevie Wednesday night. They came from the President of the United States and his committee for Employment of the Handicapped. They came from similar organizations at the state and local levels. The Michigan House of

15

Representatives gave him a special resolution of commendation.

Although Stevie is now a millionaire and the school's most famous graduate, due to his formidable musical talents — he sings, writes music, plays piano, harmonica, drums and bongos — Stevie has a mature outlook on life.

When he was honored by President Nixon at the White House last May, Stevie told the President: "The only people who are really blind are the ones whose eyes are so obscured by hatred that they can't see the light of love and justice."

That ought to be printed in braille, too. It should be printed the world over.

If I could write in braille, I'd tell Gregory Boss, salutatorian, and Bryan Howay, valedictorian, how proud folks were when they, as speakers at the ceremony, challenged themselves and their fellow graduates to "do their best," as they enter the working world of the sighted.

"We have received most of the help society can give us," Bryan said. "Now we must go out there and test our mettle."

Look out world. Here come the 1969 graduates of the Michigan School for the Blind.

Writing Wren

The secret is finally out. The wren that flew around the world sending notes back to Wisconsin sixth-graders was Wren Chadderdon.

One day last November, Chadderdon, a retired superintendent of schools, found a balloon near his home in Central Lake, Michigan. A card attached to the balloon said it had been released by a sixth-grade science class in Winneconne, Wisconsin.

The note asked the finder to send the pupils a letter telling where the balloon was found. Chadderdon, who was about to leave on a four-month trip around the world, sent the youngsters a letter that said only: "I am a bird. My name is Wren."

For the next four months, the children received letters almost every day from Wren, the bird. They came from such places as Australia, New Zealand, South Africa and England. The astounded children followed Wren's travels on the classroom globe. In the letters, Wren described the customs, food and history of each country. His letter from New Zealand even made a comparison of New Zealand's dairy industry with that of Wisconsin's.

Each letter contained a small piece of the original card that the children had attached to their balloon. As the pieces arrived, the students put the card back together.

When the last piece of puzzle came from Central Lake, the children realized where the bird, Wren, began and ended its flight. They wrote a letter to the Central Lake newspaper, and the editors uncovered Wren's identity.

Meanwhile, the sixth-graders enjoyed their most stimulating and exciting four months of school. Their knowledge of the world was broadened and the excitement made the learning process fun.

What did Chadderdon think about it all? "The winds of chance brought that balloon to me, and I couldn't resist giving those children more than they expected. Besides, it made my trip more rewarding because I could share it with the sixth-graders."

Stern Lesson

Many readers of this column probably never have heard of Brimley, let alone Brimley High School. But if you had been in the school gymnasium Saturday night, you'd have been caught up in the wonder of the place. At the end of the evening, you'd have felt better, more confident about the future of our land and its educational system.

Brimley is a tiny community on Lake Superior, about fifteen miles southwest of Sault Sainte Marie. Its high school is so small that it has a Class-D rating in athletics.

Despite that, there were more than eight hundred people at the banquet in the school gym. All were former Brimley High students. Reunions in Class-A schools don't draw crowds like that.

In the crowd were doctors, lawyers, mayors, state officials and even a former state superintendent of public instruction — a host of very successful people. The old school was popping its buttons.

As a former wearer of the Brimley Bays' blue and white, I was asked to talk at the banquet. It was easily the proudest moment of my life. I won't bore you with details because, as I said earlier, you'd have to be there to appreciate the pride of a small American community and the reverence of its people for its school.

Tears welled. I could barely talk after I mentioned my two favorite teachers, Myrtle Nelson and Karl Parker. More than eight hundred people jumped to their feet and gave those two people a long standing ovation.

Myrtle Nelson taught there for forty-four years. Parker taught algebra, coached all the athletic teams, including two state championships in basketball in 1950 and 1951.

It was an emotional moment. The evening was not meant to be a testimonial for those two great teachers, but it was a beautiful thing to behold.

Everyone, of course, has a favorite teacher. But did you ever notice that your favorite teacher was also a tough taskmaster and disciplinarian? The truth is that everyone who ever had a Nelson or a Parker class almost hated them at the time. Any fooling around in their classes meant a bop on the head with a textbook or a trip to the principal's office for punishment.

Years later, that near-hatred was transformed into pure love. Most of the people in that gym that night were wishing their children could have been taught by those two, tough old birds.

Pardon my arrogance, but I think there is a great lesson in all of this

18

— a lesson for educators everywhere. The lesson is simple enough: Children who hate tough teachers usually grow up to love them in later years.

Despite that simple truth, school administrators and parents support tough teachers less today than at any time in our history. In the past, the slap of a student's wrist used to improve citizenship and accomplishment and strengthen teacher respect. Today it would only get the teacher fired.

Before the banquet ended, Mrs. Nelson, now an elderly woman, walked to the microphone and said quietly:

"You have all kidded me over the years about how mean I was to you. But there was method to my madness. See what you have all become? I couldn't be more proud of you or of my influence. Now that you are all older, you realize that a teacher must have a very real and deep love for students in order to be a disciplinarian. Only the teachers and the parents who don't care let kids get away with bad behavior."

That brought her the second standing ovation of the night.

Are you listening, parents, teachers and administrators?

Small Is Better

Anyone who has read this column for a few years knows how I hate commencement addresses.

I have often spouted off in this space about the pompous graduation-day speakers who are long, trite and dull. They grind on and on about the torch being passed to a new generation and the youth of today being the leaders of tomorrow. The seniors sit sweating in the hot auditorium, waiting for the speech to end so they can go to the party.

So, readers, now I have a confession to make. Last week, I was a commencement speaker. I couldn't refuse. It was simply too big an honor.

The invitation came from the Whitefish Township School Board at Paradise. Speech-making has become old hat for me over the years, but I have never been more nervous at a podium than when I was addressing those thirteen kids in the Paradise graduating class.

"Don't worry about a thing, Jim," said Superintendent John Tafelski, prior to the event. "You'll be like all other speakers here. You won't be able to say much because you'll be choked up and in tears after the seniors go into the audience to present a rose to their parents. The hugs and tears out there will destroy any commencement speaker," he said.

John was right. Emotions run high at any graduation ceremony, but they are greatly heightened in a tiny school where everyone in town knows every strength and every weakness of the others. There are no secrets in a small town. Each person shares the joys and sorrows of the others.

But there are not many weaknesses in young people graduating from tiny schools like the one at Paradise. That was the theme of my talk. Most seniors from small schools enter the work world with a little feeling of inferiority. They worry that they may not be able to compete with kids graduating from bigger schools in the cities.

Not so. Seniors like those thirteen in Paradise have the world by the tail, and the sooner they realize it, the better it will be for the world. Their trump card is their attitude — and their skills are the three-R's.

Paradise seniors don't get their names in the paper, like Lansing's seniors do. Paradise has no newspaper. So, as a graduation present from the Lansing State Journal, we congratulate the following Paradise seniors:

Blake Burks, Betty Davis, Burma Davis, Amber Dennis, Julius Eggert, LeAnne Ferguson, Clayton Graham, Michael Janas, Dwaine Moore, Teri Parks, Cathy Roach, Garry Roach and Gerald Roach.

The Other Side

Forty-six Christmases have passed since I was born. I'm not sure how many I can remember, but I do know that the Christmas of 1978 is one I'll never forget.

It started great. Christmas spirit hit me early. My son Steve flew home from Denver, where he is attending an automotive school. Linda, now a junior at MSU, was also home. That was exciting. For my wife Darl and me, those "kids" are our life.

A day or two after Steve arrived, I was in my basement workshop, tinkering with something, when he came up behind me and grabbed me in a playful father-son wrestling session. When I turned to look at him, his eyes were dimmed with tears.

"I missed you, Dad," he said. I never heard four greater words in my forty-six years. Christmas does that. It's a time for families to reunite and fight lumps in throats.

Then, things went downhill. Sunday, Christmas Eve, arrived and Linda became ill. In desperation, we took her to Ingham Medical Hospital's emergency room. While Linda waited in the long line of sick and injured people, Steve, Darl and I spent several restless hours.

A man next to me began to cry. I offered him comfort, asking what was wrong.

"We just brought my mother here," he said. "She has severe pains in her stomach and she is old...This is Christmas Eve, and...last year on Christmas Eve, my father died. God save us from another Christmas like that," he sobbed.

My heart went out to that man and, as I wiped away tears of my own, I heard the wail of ambulance sirens. Steve and I watched as the paramedics rushed a man on a stretcher into the emergency room. They were vigorously thumping his chest as they passed us.

"Heart attack victim, cardiac arrest," I heard one of the office workers say.

Time passed and a doctor called me into a room where Linda was being examined.

"Take her to Sparrow Hospital right away," he said. "She has an infection and a fever. We'll have to admit her and do some tests."

"Wow, there goes Christmas," said Linda through tears. There were four glum faces on the Hough family as we got ready to leave.

Then, a doctor called several members of another family from the waiting room and said, "I'm sorry. He's gone. We did all we could." It was the heart attack victim brought in minutes earlier. The sobs of

21

the man's sons, daughters and wife will live with me forever.

Suddenly, Linda's problems seemed so minor. Surely, by comparison, they were. She spent Christmas Eve in the hospital, and we were worried and depressed, but a happy note was sounded by the doctor on Christmas morning: "Linda can come home right away," he said. We rushed to get her.

Finally, it was like other Christmases. We were around the tree and the fireplace, opening gifts. Happy times had returned.

But there was one more 1978 "downer" for Steve and me. We went to keep our noon appointment at the Volunteers of America offices downtown, where we annually deliver hot Christmas meals to the elderly and shut-ins. We were given the name of an elderly woman living alone on Lansing's northeast side.

We knocked on the door of her modest home for a long time before we heard movement inside. After a struggle, she opened the door. Then we saw the reason for her slow movement. The woman, dressed in an old flannel shirt that had belonged to her husband, peered out at us and with difficulty, moved her walker and opened her door.

We told her we were delivering a hot Christmas dinner from the Volunteers of America. Pride straightened those tiny, bent shoulders, and she protested, but Steve and I convinced her to take the meal.

We laid the hot meat out at her kitchen table and prepared to leave. "Merry Christmas," we told her.

She looked at us for a moment and then broke into tears. Although my reporter efficiency was never at a lower level than at that moment, I remember a few of the things she said:

"Oh, I hear that so often this time of year — have a Merry Christmas — but they are empty words for me. Christmas can never be merry for me again. New Year's Eve is the worst for me. That's when my husband died. I had him for fifty-three years. There is nothing to live for now.

"I'm old and I can't even do my own vacuuming. My home is a mess. I have no relatives here. The next thing is that I will lose my home to the government. I can't pay the taxes anymore.

"I don't think people care about old people anymore. I called several places recently to find some church group or an individual who would take me to my doctor appointment. Finally, I had to cancel it. I could not afford the taxi fare, let alone the doctor bill," she said.

On several occasions, I urged her to eat her meal before it got cold. But it finally struck me: The meal was not important to her. Having visitors who cared was a far more important Christmas Day event for her. Steve and I stayed, and although her meal got cold, we learned a lot about what it means to be old and alone.

We hardly spoke as we returned home. I felt bad, afraid I had overdone my do-gooder role and brought a special depression to my son's Christmas.

"Sorry, son. We've had a lousy Christmas this year," I said, as we parked the car in our garage.

He paused a long moment before he responded. "Well, we sure saw a lot of the other side, didn't we, Dad? I mean, Christmas is not always a happy time for people. I don't think I will ever forget that old lady," he said.

"Our family is awfully lucky, Dad," Steve said as he slammed the car door.

"Amen," I said.

Herman Meets Human

[Editor's Note: This was the first of many conversations between Jim Hough and Herman, the Mexican burro. Later interviews with Herman led to the establishment of Lansing's Friends of the Zoo Society. That organization has since raised nearly one million dollars for Potter Park Zoo improvements.]

"By golly, Jim, this is the first time I've been interviewed by a reporter. I'm really impressed."

That was the opening comment of Herman, the Mexican burro who has delighted visitors to the Potter Park Zoo for nearly twenty years, when I went there to interview him.

I didn't go there to ask him what he thinks of such things as urban renewal, parking ramps, Jaycees or Dick McAuliffe's batting stance. I questioned Herman about his life at the zoo.

"Well, I'm eighteen years old now, and some guys around here say I'm living on borrowed time," Herman said. "Maybe I have outlived the average burro, but I've had a pretty soft life. I sometimes get letters from burros in Mexico who have to work for a living."

I was about to ask a question when Herman interrupted: "Excuse me a minute. I see a boy at the fence with a carrot. Carrots are my favorite."

Plodding back to the center of his pen, where I was seated in a comfortable chair with my clipboard, Herman grinned and said: "Don't quote me on this, Jim, because I don't want the gestapo around here to know it, but there is one lady who comes here every week with a pound of carrots for me. And another person brings me sugar cubes, a pound at a time."

The interview continued:

How do you keep in good health while eating so promiscuously, Herman?

"What does that 'promiscuously' stuff mean?"

What I mean is, how come you don't get sick or something?

"Oh, yeh. Well, I do get sick a lot."

What did you do before you came to the zoo here, Herman?

"Well, that is kind of a mystery to me. I don't remember too much of my early years. They say I was born on an airplane, while my mother was being flown from South America to the United States to perform in the Shriner circus. I first came to Lansing when I was bought by the late Henry Owens, who used me as a Shriner mascot. I flew all over the country.

"But, one of the wildest things they ever did with me was when those guys who used to have a car agency on East Michigan Avenue

24

put me in a little car with a hole in the roof. They paraded me all over town, trying to sell those special hole-in-the-roof cars. I don't think they sold that many, but I got a lot of carrots out of it. Carrots are my favorite food. You can quote me on that.''

Workers at the zoo say you are spoiled, Herman. Do you think they baby you too much?

"Now what kind of question is that? You reporters pry a lot. What business is that of yours? I take the Fifth Amendment on that!''

Do you really like children, Herman, or do you just butter them up, so you can get fresh carrots?

"I was starting to like you, Jim, till you started to get so personal. I suppose I do sort of take advantage of the kids sometimes. But, you'd be surprised what a kid will give up just to scratch my ears once.''

Herman, the way you eat, it's a wonder you don't have an ulcer.

"Yeh, but I have to make it good while the tourist season is on. You know these guys here put me on a diet every fall and make me lose about forty pounds. They say it's not healthy for me to be so heavy. They cut me down to hay, oats and a few carrots. It's miserable.

"But, during the summer, I get fed popcorn, kernel corn, candy, potato chips, chewing gum, cigarettes, and sometimes even a good chunk of chewing tobacco. I like that stuff a lot, but I'm not addicted to it like a lot of burros. And if I was, I'd quit. They say that stuff will give you cancer.''

How do you figure you rate as a public attraction here, Herman?

"Well, sir, Mr. Hough, that is one of the big bugaboos of my life to-day. For many years, I was number one here and, boy, could I ever call the shots then. But, three years ago, they got that cursed chimp, Adam. Now, they say, he ranks first. I don't know whose rating services they use, but I want to tell you that that chimp just doesn't have it as far as I am concerned. All he ever does is spit on people and thump around in his cell like a maniac. He sometimes reminds me of Castro making a five-hour speech. But, if people like to go and be spit on by a chimp, well, that's the way it goes.''

Herman, how come you never bray when there are people near your pen?

"Now, listen buddy,'' whispered Herman, "don't quote me on this, but I have a system I use in braying. I wait until everybody is down watching those crazy monkeys or in watching that dirty chimp spit on people, and then I really cut loose with my best brays. It gets attention focused back here, where it belongs.

"Heck, Jim, a lot of people come here just to see me. They come and scratch my ears, give me carrots, and then leave without even glancing at another animal. I wish somebody would tell that chimp that. Does he think he's something!''

You ought to learn some tricks, Herman, and maybe you could get top billing again.

"Oh, no, none of that stuff for me. They tried to teach me to shake

25

hands. I did it, too, for a week. Then I saw what kind of a deal that would turn into, so I quit. I haven't shaken a hand in ten years. I don't have to do that stuff. Maybe, though, I should start spitting on folks."

Do you get good treatment from the zoo workers, Herman?

"Oh, you bet I do. Don't let these guys kid you about me being spoiled. They love me to death. That Bill Swix, who gives me my hay and oats, sometimes just hugs me for the heck of it. They all love me here."

Since you are getting so old, Herman, do you ever think about the day you won't be here anymore?

"Oh, I've had a good life and a long one. My ears have been scratched by a million kids, I guess. Some of those who scratched my head when they were little tots are now grown up and have children of their own. How many old donkeys are there in the world who have made so many children so happy?

"My best reward here came once when a youngster pal of mine risked his neck for me. About four years ago, six boys came to the zoo at night, carrying sticks with nails in them. They killed a kangaroo and a deer before they got to my pen. They beat me up and cut me badly. It was awful.

"But, some time later, a boy went to the police. He was not one of the mean boys who hit me, but he said he knew who the boys were. He told the police that he loved me. The boys then were caught and punished. That boy can scratch my ears anytime.

"It's a great life here. I still have good hearing and sight, and I get around well. I may live for many years yet. One guy here told me I didn't dare die because it would make too many kids cry. He said it would be one of the biggest funerals ever held hereabouts."

It certainly would, Herman. I don't know of a child in Lansing who wouldn't be there.

Grandfather Clause

I have a fantastic idea for an Onlooker contest. I want to be the first to enter it.

Who became the first first-time grandfather in Lansing at 7:34 a.m. Friday, February 25? We haven't had that much excitement at the Onlooker desk since an Eaton Rapids farmer dumped a sack of four-pound potatoes on it. It's a girl, Caitlin Neve Cornell, eight pounds, three ounces, at St. Lawrence Hospital.

When my loud, happy yell came from the Onlooker desk as I hung up the phone (a call from my son-in-law Bob Cornell), I looked up to see Hal Fildey, executive editor (big boss in the newsroom), standing over me.

"OK, Jim, I am now giving you an executive order. Based on your bad track record with columns on the Upper Peninsula and baseball, I hereby decree that you are limited to one grandchild column per month," he said.

I launched an immediate protest: "Hold on, Hal. We're going to renegotiate my contract. I want a grandfather clause in there."

My daughter Linda had been married two years, and I was beginning to worry. "Look, Linda, I said nine months ago, "I think you ought to have kids as soon as you can afford them. If you can't afford them, let me know. I want a grandchild."

So, her pregnancy was a major event. I have been bugging Linda almost daily for several months, urging her to hurry up the process. She got weary of my pestering her.

Friday morning I was awakened by the phone. "Good morning, Dad," Linda said. "Since you have been bugging me so much for so long, I thought I'd call you to let you know I'm leaving for the hospital. It's 3 a.m., Dad. Good night, I hope you sleep well." She hung up.

I guess I had that coming. No prospective grandparent was ever more awake at 3 a.m. — and stayed that way.

Now, I will take about five hundred pictures of the baby. I want to show them to all those grandparents who have bored me over the years by showing me endless strings of pictures of their grandchildren. It's getting-even time.

Surely, there is something very special about the role of grandparents. My wife Darl and I only hope we are worthy. Get ready for the most spoiled grandchild in Lansing history.

Tradition Dies

We had a great Christmas, as usual. But, sadly, the 1975 version might be the last of a long and beautiful Christmas tradition for the Hough family in its northern, wintry Paradise.

It all began many years ago, when our kids were small. Now, Linda is a high school senior, and Steve is a sophomore.

In those days, our snug, little cabin on the shore of Lake Superior's Whitefish Bay near Paradise was hidden a mile away from a plowed road and even farther away from a neighbor.

Darl, my wife, and I used to put on snowshoes, load the kids, groceries and boxes of Christmas presents on toboggans, and then make the trip to the cabin — walking down a trail bounded by beautiful, snow-covered pines. When she was about ten, Linda once observed that the pines seemed to be wearing white lace. Oh, those were beautiful moments...the crunch of the snowshoes, in the silence of a beautiful winter swamp.

In those days, our only cabin conveniences were an outside pitcher pump and an outhouse. Inside was a Franklin stove, which old dad had to feed every two hours all night long, to keep the place from turning into a deep freeze.

But we kept warm with more than the heat generated from the Franklin stove.

There was a special family warmth — a time when the kids seemed to enjoy climbing up in our laps, a time when we all seemed to notice each other more than usual. We talked to each other, and we listened to each other.

This year wasn't much different in those respects. We still had the family warmth and lots of fun — snowshoe walks in the woods, night bonfires and ice-skating parties and feeding the Franklin stove.

But, the cabin has inside plumbing now and a gas furnace. This winter, for the first time, the county crews are plowing out the road to our cabin. The neighbors are closer now, and many of them live there year-round.

However, that's not the worst of it. The worst is that our kids are growing up. On our return to Lansing this week, they said they had had the best Christmas yet, and that they wanted to do it again next year.

But Darl and I know that is unlikely. Linda will be graduated from high school and probably busy with college and boyfriends. We know it will be tough to get everyone together for a week-long Christmas trip to Paradise next year.

I'm reminded of the lyrics in a country music song: "Don't cry, Mama, birds and children fly away."

Black and White Tears

Eleven black men, many from far-away cities, came to honor a white man for something he did a quarter-century ago.

The white man is Col. Frank S. Pritchard, a retired army colonel and retired state editor of The State Journal.

The black men are former officers in the all-Negro 614th Tank Destroyer Battalion, which distinguished itself in some bloody World War II battles, in the rush from Normandy to German soil.

Col. Pritchard was their leader, their friend, their champion. Of the battalion's seven hundred men and thirty-five officers, only five were white.

I heard those eleven black men sing praises of Pritchard Saturday night in Detroit, at a banquet that was as warm and touching as any I had ever attended.

The black men recalled that Col. Pritchard was tough, demanding and courageous. But what they talked most about was his giant contribution to the black man's course of civil rights. They told about how he was fair to them. They told of how he constantly fought the army's white establishment on their behalf.

When the banquet ceremonies were closing, and it was time for Col. Pritchard to speak, the short, slightly built, balding man stood erect and began in his rough, authoritative voice:

"I didn't make the battalion what it was; you men did that. You were the finest soldiers I ever commanded in all my years in the army...I can't go on...I love you, men. I love you."

The tough old colonel sat down, and he sobbed openly and loudly. And every man in the room cried with him.

They were black. He was white. The tears were the same color. They came from a rare kind of love.

It was World War II, and it was a time when civil rights was not much of an issue. It was a time when white men said that black men would not fight in combat. It was a time when black troops were assigned to run motor pools and man the kitchens.

But, when Col. Pritchard was asked to command and train a Negro battalion, he agreed on one condition — that all his officers be black. He didn't quite accomplish that end, but thirty of his thirty-five officers were black.

In combat, the 614th gained one Distinguished Service Cross, eight Silver Stars, forty Bronze Stars and a host of other commendations. One platoon received a Presidential Citation for a particularly vicious fight, the account of which is printed in the book, "The Hundred Best Stories from Stars and Stripes."

Charles Thomas, of Detroit, black commander of one of the battalion's four companies, became the second Negro soldier in American history to receive the Distinguished Service Cross. Capt. Thomas, although wounded three times and bleeding badly, continued to lead a charge of his men that successfully fought off a German tank attack.

Dr. Thomas M. Campbell, himself a retired colonel and a pediatrician at Tuskegee Institute in Alabama, was the first black officer transferred to Pritchard's new outfit.

"I never trusted white men," Dr. Campbell said at the banquet. "I never had much reason to trust them, until I met Frank Pritchard. I soon trusted him and loved him. He is a truly great man."

Ulysses W. Watkins, retired lieutenant colonel and now director of education for military personnel at St. Louis, Mo., said:

"Three men gave me my motivation, guidance and inspiration in life — my father, a school principal and Col. Pritchard. But, the colonel most of all, because he gave me what black men want most, self-respect."

Dr. Campbell recalled that Pritchard told the men he wanted soldiers, not a race of people. "He instilled such pride and dedication in all of us that we never talked or thought about racial differences," the doctor said.

Retired Maj. Robert S. Williams, now a U.S. Treasury agent in Washington, D.C., said:

"Col. Pritchard had men who would go to hell with him. I was one of them. The loyalty between us and the colonel was not just a thing that flowed from us to him. It flowed down from him as well. He made a special point of knowing the weaknesses and strengths of his men...When I got out of the service in 1951, one of my first acts was to go and visit Col. Pritchard."

Forest Walker, retired lieutenant colonel, who is now an official in the Oldsmobile personnel division in Lansing, said, "Col. Pritchard, this is a pilgrimage. A pilgrimage to show the respect, love and pride we have for you. We are here to honor you, a man who did some mighty important things for the Negro cause in the pre-civil rights days."

There was more than serious talk at the gathering, however. The men came to the Detroit hotel Friday afternoon, and they talked well into the night. Pritchard went to bed at 4:30 a.m., and the men had him up again at 7:30 a.m., as they relived some of their proudest, funniest and saddest days in World War II.

The men told of the time they stole some pigs from a German farm and began a pig barbecue. The colonel walked by, and the men thought they were in trouble. But, he sliced off a chunk of pork, ate it and passed on with the comment, "Bury the bones deep, men."

The men once "liberated" eighteen hundred bottles of French

champagne. Instead of objecting, Pritchard ordered that two bottles be given to each enlisted man in the battalion.

Frank Pritchard's balding head reddened a little as he heard one of his men say, "The colonel was sort of a poor man's Abe Lincoln to us."

Then, Pritchard's rough voice returned to dominate the scene: "Look, enough of that. We lived, ate, worked and fought together for three years. I never thought of you men as black. I hope you never thought of me as white."

A silence struck the room before Col. Pritchard continued, "And now, I've heard enough praise of the old man. Somebody get me a drink."

Eleven black men stumbled over themselves, rushing to obey the colonel's command.

A Chance To Excel

Hey, wait a minute, these kids aren't mentally retarded. I must be on the wrong bus.

That was the thought I had a few minutes after I got on a school bus taking thirty-three Alabama youngsters to Mt. Pleasant, where they will participate in the Special Olympics. The youngsters were among Alabama's seventy-eight olympic athletes, who had just arrived at Capital City Airport.

"Who are you?" asked the lad on the seat next to me.

I introduced myself and asked his name.

"I'm Booker T. Rutledge. I'm from Birmingham. We've got a basketball team — eight of us are right here. See our red jackets and blue shirts? We got a great team. Our coach said we can beat any team in the world," he said excitedly.

Wow. And this boy is retarded?

"Booker gets more fouls than he gets points," chided Daryl Lee, fifteen, of Tuscaloosa, a two-hundred-twenty-yard-dash specialist.

There was laughter from Booker's teammates. Good, fun laughter — the kind you hear when you are around any high school basketball team.

It shook me. I was expecting halting speech and dull, confused answers. I went to the front of the bus and introduced myself to the man who seemed to be in charge. I told him of my surprise.

The lined face of sixty-three-year-old Charles Stapp, vice chairman of the Alabama Special Olympics and director of the state Department of Education's physical education program, looked at me and his smile broadened.

"That's the beauty of the Special Olympics. It teaches many, many people — including newspaper reporters — that a slow learner is not necessarily an abnormal person. Seeing you react that way is my first big thrill on this trip. That's what it's all about," he said.

While I sat there, amid my confusion and embarrassment, Stapp went on with his gentle lecture:

"I guess every child on this bus has an I.Q. rating below seventy, but you have just seen that an I.Q. of seventy can bring a lot of learning, if we give it time and special patience. Every time we drill that point home to a newspaperman like you, we feel a thrill.

"I have had a lot of thrills in my life. I was a state track champion when I was a boy, and I was a teammate of Bear Bryant on Alabama's 1934 Rose Bowl team. But my biggest thrills come from watching these youngsters teach people something about the nature of mental retardation. Why don't you go and talk with the kids some more?"

Billy Lammert, a seventeen-year-old from Birmingham, had pride and emotion in his face as he told me that he will compete in the free-style and breast-stroke swim events.

"I have the number. I'm going to call my parents on the telephone Saturday. They want to know if I won a gold medal. I think I can win a gold medal. And I want to tell them about the airplane, too. That was fun."

Only two of the seventy-eight youngsters in the delegation had ever been on an airplane before yesterday. Most of them considered it a great thrill — except fifteen-year-old Wallace Morris, of Jasper, Ala.

"I was scared," he said. "I didn't like the airplane." Wallace will compete in bowling and has won a state medal for his three-hundred-ninety-one score in a three-game series.

Harold Gooden, a sixteen-year-old from Birmingham, reached across the aisle and tugged at my arm.

"I do the high jump. I can jump five feet and one inch. I won two gold medals already. I think they are nice. I keep them on the wall by my bed. My dad wants to come here to see me jump, but he can't. It's far away to Alabama, isn't it?"

It was starting to get me — that old lump in the throat. I returned to the front of the bus to take refuge in another gentle lecture from Stapp.

"I have watched the Special Olympics do great things for our educational program," Stapp said. "It has done wonders to open the eyes of the world. Each year, we find the governor and state legislature more receptive to new educational programs for the retarded."

A boy of about sixteen paused in the aisle and put his hand on Stapp's shoulder. Stapp gripped the boy's hand in both of his. The lad then continued down the aisle.

"One thing you learn very quickly in working with the mentally retarded is that they are far more lovable and affectionate than other kids," Stapp said. "Sometimes you can thrill them simply by putting your arm around them. And that shouldn't surprise anybody. After all, they may have the body of a teen-ager, but in mind they may be just a small child. What small child do you know who does not thrill to the embrace of a mother, father or a friend?"

Stapp continued, "All they need is a chance to excel among their peers. That will do more to get them into the mainstream of society than anything else — but don't forget to add lots of love as you offer them this chance to compete."

The bus stopped. It was at the end of the line. It seemed as if I had just got on. I turned to leave, but paused to wave to the kids. I wished them good luck, and said I would cheer for them.

The bowler, Wallace Morris, stood up in front of me and offered his hand for a shake. I took the hand, looked into his face for a moment, and then turned to step down from the bus.

The lump in my throat was back again.

Roasting a Friend

Jim Decker always said he hated retirement parties. "Too much like funerals," he'd say.

So, it was not surprising that he fought off efforts of his fellow secretary of state employees to have a retirement party honoring him for his thirty-three years of service.

Jim, whose real name is Warren, is just about the closest friend I have. He is a former state police trooper. He has been a secretary of state field office representative at Mt. Pleasant for many years.

I talked him into attending the retirement party Saturday night at the Pretzel Bell restaurant. I told him I would be a speaker there, and I promised to keep it light-hearted. Nothing serious. That, we both knew, would not be easy. Jim and I are made of the same stuff. We cry easily. We are emotional softies.

For instance, I'd cry whenever he sang his favorite song, "That Silver-Haired Daddy of Mine." Jim lost his father when he was a young lad. Remember the Red Foley song, "Old Shep"? Jim always cried when he heard that song because he once had a dog named Shep. The sad, old country tune always had him reaching for his handkerchief.

Jim has always been a practical joker. So, I kept his retirement party light-hearted by recounting some of his crazy antics. There was the time he bought a discarded printing press and tried to deposit it in my garage when I wasn't home. There was the time he caught a big dogfish and then wired it to the springs of my car. It was June, and there was a week of terrible odor before I found out.

There was the time he ran over a fox on the road and then crept to my car in the night to stuff the dead fox inside a hubcap. That was July. I found the source of that odor when the bones began rattling around in the hubcap.

And there was the time one winter when he knew we were away for the weekend. He tried to enter our house through a window. His plan was to fill the bathtub with Jello. A neighbor called the police. He had a tough time explaining his way out of that one.

There was the time I caught a huge trout in the first few minutes on a fishing trip in Canada. Jim netted the fish for me and then calmly pulled out his knife, cut the line and tossed the fish into the lake.

"I'm the leader on this trip, and I get to catch the first fish," he said. I've never been so aghast in my life.

There was the time we played cribbage under a gasoline lantern light near our tent on a Canadian island. We were on a cliff, high above the water. As I whipped him for the sixth straight game, he calmly reached for the deck and the cribbage board and threw them out into the lake.

He stomped into the tent and crawled into his sleeping bag. I turned out the light and entered the tent. I zipped the tent flap and crawled into my sleeping bag.

A few hours later, I heard a yell and a sound of ripping canvas. Jim had run right through the side of the tent. I had forgotten about his claustrophobia when I had closed up the tent, leaving no light showing. Man, he nearly ran right off that cliff.

I also told everyone at the retirement party about the many, many instances of intestinal disturbance suffered by Jim when he ate his favorite food — my wife's egg salad sandwiches with onion bread.

The laughter was strong at that gathering. I could have told Jim Decker stories all night. But, I quit. Just before I left the speaker's stand, I reached down and punched the play button on a tape recorder, which I had hidden there. The recorder played ''Old Shep.''

I tossed a box of Kleenex to Jim. Yes, I know it was a dirty trick, but he deserved it after all he had done to me. The tears welled up in his eyes. I cried, too. They say it was quite a show.

But, borrowing a quote from the great Hank Williams, it was ''a happy kind of sadness.'' I've also had a million laughs with that great man.

I was contacted this week by Tom Martin, Mt. Pleasant police chief, and Don Gillis, Isabella County sheriff. They said they are planning another retirement party for Jim at Mt. Pleasant on February 1. They asked if I would be master of ceremonies. Just think, Jim, we get to do it all over again.

Put in a double order for Kleenex.

A Tougher Job

My heart goes out to the wives of policemen.

Many of my closest friends are policemen. I don't know why. Maybe it's because reporters and policemen have a lot in common and are forced to work together under stressful conditions.

I sat in the newsroom Thursday, with my ear to the police radio monitor, as the bank holdup took place. I listened and the tension grew. When I heard that plain-clothes officers from the organized crime unit were called to the scene, I knew that my buddy and neighbor, Sgt. Ray Morris, was there.

When a voice on the radio blurted anxiously, "The subjects are in custody...an officer is down...send an ambulance," I felt a deep pit in my stomach.

I looked up to see Chris Wells, State Journal librarian, standing there. Her husband is an East Lansing policeman. The radio had noted earlier that East Lansing police were on the scene.

An eternity passed and the episode developed. I sat in a bustling and frantic newsroom as the facts unfolded.

Later, my phone rang. It was Sgt. Morris. In a broken voice he said, "Jim, see if you can find Winnie. Tell her I'm OK. I can't reach her by phone. Thanks, I've got to go now...God, Jim, he was one of my men. We stood there — saw it all — couldn't do a damned thing. It was too late. Those five kids..." He sobbed as he hung up the phone.

Winnie, Ray's wife, is employed at the State Journal. We ride to work together daily.

But, of course, that was not the worst of it. The worst came for Margaret Donnelly, wife of Officer Mac Donnelly, Jr. She had to be told that her husband was dead.

Lt. William Cochran and Officer Phyllis Baker drew that assignment. They would have to tell Mrs. Donnelly that her husband was shot by a gunman, as he made a heroic attempt to save hostages in a bank robbery.

"I'd rather have taken the bullet myself, than face her with that news," Cochran told me later.

They found Mrs. Donnelly at the Impression Five Museum. Until then, it had been a happy day for the Donnellys. They had learned earlier that their new motor home had arrived, and that they would be able to pick it up that night. To ease the excitement, Mrs. Donnelly had taken her children on a tour of the museum.

Yeah, it's tough being a policeman, but I wonder if it isn't a bit tougher to be the wife of a policeman.

Nixon's Adventures

The regular writer of this "Off the Road" column, Mark Nixon, is on the road vacationing with his family. So, it seems a perfect opportunity to write an "Off the Road" about the "Off the Road" writer.

Because Mark has written dozens of these columns, calling attention to the strange behavior of others — like the man who drinks beer while standing on his head, and the man who rides a motorcycle around with a bird on his head — I think it is time readers learned of the strange behavior that characterizes Mark Nixon.

Mark is a walking disaster. His father says Mark has always been as clumsy as a cub bear. Recently, Mark came into the newsroom wearing a large, red scar on the end of his nose. After intense interrogation, we got a confession from him.

"I burned it on a shovel," he said. "I was burning some trash and poking around in the fire with the shovel. Later, I smelled something strange, and it seemed to be coming from the shovel. I put the metal up to smell it, and I burned my nose."

Another time, Mark came into the newsroom with a large bump on his head. Under heavy interrogation once again, he confessed that he had been working on a ladder at his home and had hung his hammer on a rung of the ladder. Later, he moved the ladder, and you know what then happened to the hammer.

In the newsroom, Mark is continually dropping things. The worst is when he rushes to his desk to pick up the ringing phone and then drops the receiver, letting it crash to the desk and then to the floor. We have often wondered how many readers he has deafened that way.

As Mark stands talking with you, he usually is nervously jingling the keys to his Toyota truck. We timed him once, and he dropped the keys on the floor four times in five minutes.

And there was the time he got the big bump on his head when he sneezed...standing in front of a urinal.

And there was the time he drove down Kalamazoo Street during a flood, and his car went into the Red Cedar River. The last Mark saw of it, it was floating slowly downstream. Later, he recovered the car. It had a ticket on it. He was charged with blocking a highway.

And there was the time Mark bought a new freezer for his home and then feared it would not go down his basement stairway. He got the measurements of the freezer and then built a framework of boards in that size.

He then asked his wife to help him maneuver the freezer mockup down the stairs. About two steps down, the whole thing collapsed into a dozen pieces. Mark, who has a fine sense of humor, did not laugh along with his wife and their two children, Ryanne and Andy.

But, Mark's biggest cub-bear act came recently, at the Calkins Paint Store on East Michigan Avenue. He went there to buy a quart of varnish. Mark stood in the store, holding the quart of varnish and talking with one of the clerks. Suddenly, he dropped the can. The lid popped open, and the varnish spilled out over the shoes of the store clerk. That was not the worst of it. The varnish also spilled on a carpet and immediately melted the carpet backing.

Mark offered to buy another quart of varnish. ''You just bought the last quart we had,'' the clerk said.

While all of the above is true, there is more to Mark than his bear-cub act. As some readers may know, I write the Onlooker column in this newspaper, and I wish I had a nickel for each letter I have received complimenting Mark's writing and reporting.

I share their admiration for him.

Charlie's Run

For bus driver Charlie Buhs and his passengers, Friday was the end of the line.

After fourteen years with Lansing Suburban Lines, Charlie, forty-two, was forced into an early retirement because his vision has been impaired by glaucoma.

Charlie's final trip on the South Cedar run found this reporter talking to many of Charlie's long-time passengers, many of whom wiped away tears without embarrassment.

"Gee, Charlie, I guess I won't ever see you again," were the emotion-choked words of Mrs. Edna Fields, as she started to get off the bus.

She had fiddled with her handkerchief earlier, as she told of how Charlie was always especially kind to older folks.

"You are certainly a wonderful person," said another elderly woman, as Charlie left the wheel to help her into the bus.

The praise was genuine and so were the tears. But, what's so special about this guy Buhs?

Well, not much except that he leaves a legacy of many kind acts along the South Cedar route, which has hundreds of customers and friends buzzing about him.

There were about eight of Charlie's regular customers on the bus when I boarded it. I asked them why they liked Charlie.

"Oh, there are not enough words," said elderly Mrs. O.T. Kinney. She paused to use her handkerchief and then went on to recall how Charlie had done such kind things as to help women with their shopping bags, send most of his customers Christmas cards and visit them when they were in the hospital. Once, she said, he even stopped to help an elderly woman shovel her walk, so she could get to the bus.

What folks think of Charlie was demonstrated last week, when he was asked to visit one of his customers on Alpha Street. As he walked in the door, thirty-six children and ten adults yelled, "Surprise!"

They had bought a huge cake in the shape of a city bus. They gave him a briefcase to use in his new job as a salesman for a roofing company.

"I never saw a guy like him," said Leon Stevens. "I have been a rider on his bus for several years. Twice, when I was in the hospital, Charlie visited me. It sort of makes you feel real good inside when a guy takes time out for a kindness like that."

The bus rolled on. Children waved from nearly every corner.

"Charlie!" they yelled.

"Boy, will I miss those guys," Buhs tried to say, through the lump in his throat.

But they will miss him more. In recent years, Charlie has taken the children on a special tour at Christmas, to show them the city's decorations.

"Last year, there were fifty-seven youngsters," he said. "I gave them all a treat. The first year, I rented the bus for the project. But after that, the company thought it was a nice thing, and they furnished the equipment free."

Once, when Buhs was hospitalized, some children along Alpha Street took up a collection and bought him a plant for his room.

About two hundred people boarded his bus daily. He knows about ninety percent of them by their first names. He said he received forty Christmas gifts last year from passengers.

"This eye trouble is causing me a lot of concern," Charlie said. "My doctors say I just can't keep on as a bus driver. My problem is that the glaucoma was in the advanced stages before it was detected.

"I will have to keep working at another job though, because I have three daughters, who are eighteen, fourteen and thirteen, and they are at the expensive stage. One is in college," he said.

Carl Buchanan, an official of the Lansing Suburban Lines, said, "I have never met a more loyal employee. I am saddened that he cannot stay with us. Chuck is the most outstanding employee I have ever met, and the company will surely miss him. We have never had a complaint about him, just many nice compliments. He treats people like they are entitled to be treated."

Passenger Abe Haddad had misty eyes when he turned to me, just before getting off the bus downtown. "Chuck's eyes are damaged," he said, "but his heart and his brain are not blind. He is a wonderful man."

40

Felling a Widowmaker

It was the late innings of a close ballgame between the Tigers and Toronto. I stared intently at the TV screen in my living room. The phone rang in the kitchen. Frustrated, I went to answer it.

"Hi, Jim, this is Weave," said the voice of MSU Athletic Director Doug Weaver.

"This must be a big emergency, if you are calling in the eighth inning of a tie game," I grumbled.

"It is an emergency," he said. "It's a long story, but it all started a couple of weeks ago, when my daughter, Amy, got married, and we had a big reception here at the house. Shortly after that, the septic tank quit working. I've had several consultants out here, and they tell me I have to replace my septic tank and drain field..."

I halted Doug and said, "Hold on, you and I are woodcuttters, not sewage technicians."

"That's just it, Jim. It is because of our Paul-Bunyan-and-Babe-the-Blue-Ox act that I'm calling. See, the problem is that there is a giant oak tree right where the new drain field has to go, and they say the tree has to be removed. After all the bragging you and I have done about our timber cutting and wood chopping, I'm embarrassed to call in an expert. I figure we'll have to do it.

"I just read the first paragraph in my tree-felling book, and it says amateurs shouldn't do it. The book calls such trees 'widowmakers.' The question is, Jim, do we have the guts to do it or not? What if word got around town that Hough and Weaver were chicken to cut down a tree?"

"OK, OK, Doug. I'll come out, and we'll make a study of the tree," I agreed.

It was a monster oak. A chill went up my spine as I looked at it. "It's gonna take a lot of Strohs to get that bugger down," I observed.

Meanwhile, our wives, Darl and Nancy, stood by, arguing against the venture. Darl told of her friend who had become a widow when her husband tried to cut down a tree in the front yard. We didn't want to hear that kind of talk, so we told the women to take Barney (Doug's dog) and go hide in the basement, where they'd be safe.

We eyed the tree some more. We figured it could only fall in one small path without smashing up the neighbor's property or getting hung up in other trees.

"Well, Jim, should we call in an expert and then take a verbal beating from our friends?" Doug asked. I think he hoped I'd say, "Yes."

I grabbed my chain saw, cranked 'er up and began making the falling notch. That done, I motioned Doug and his son Matt to a safe area behind me, and I began to cut through that giant tree. Fortunately, the roar of the saw covered up the loud heartbeats in my chest.

There was a cracking, the tree tilted slightly and then fell with a great crash that must have been heard all the way to Howell. Perfect! We put 'er right on a dime.

Doug ran up to hug me. "You just got a standing ovation," he said.

I hoped Doug and Matt would not see the trembling in my hands, as I put down the chain saw.

But, I gave it all away as I tried to light up a celebratory cigar. My trembling fingers couldn't get the match near the end of the cigar.

Our legend is intact, but my nerves are shot.

Now, full of confidence, Doug has his eye on a much bigger, dead oak tree in his woodlot. "Heck, Jim, we can cut that one down. She'd make some great firewood."

"No way," I said. "For that one, we're calling my veterinarian buddy, Dr. Jack Grounds. He has two things we need greatly — more guts and a bigger chain saw."

Leaving a Mark

John Ward is the Lansing State Journal's news editor and regular author of this Sunday column. I asked for this space today because John is in Ohio, grieving the loss of his father, Edward Ward.

This column has high readership, and I am proud to say here that John has been one of my dearest friends for many years. Perhaps you'll give me a moment to tell you some things about John's father. They will help you understand some things about John.

Lima, Ohio, is a city of about fifty thousand people. For many years, Ed Ward has been referred to there as "Mr. Lima." He died February 25, at eighty-one, having been in ill health for several months.

I was there for the funeral last Wednesday. I found myself standing taller and straighter because I had known him. Hundreds came — mayors, school superintendents and hordes of common folks.

Many told John that they had worked for his father. When John told them he always understood that his dad was tough to work for, most answered this way: "No, he was not hard to work for. It's just that he meant what he said." Respect for the man poured out of the people of Lima. They loved him dearly.

One woman came to the funeral from quite a distance. She went to the open casket and cried. Nobody knew her. John introduced himself and the woman said, "I admired him so. When I was a young girl, I was kicked around from one foster home to another. Mr. Ward gave me a job. He was the first real gentleman I ever met in my life. I have not seen him in many years, but I could never forget him."

Funerals are sad occasions for sure. But you can easily see why that one filled the Ward family with such pride. Men who make that kind of a mark in their lives don't really die.

An unusual thing happened Tuesday morning, as I hurried to get out Onlooker columns and leave town to attend that funeral. The first letter I opened in that morning's mail was from Linda Smalley, of Mason. She enclosed an anonymous poem, which had been sent to her on the occasion of her father's death. She said it gave her great comfort, and she wanted to share it with others who might be grieving. The poem surely fits the passing of Edward Ward. It reads:

> Do not stand by my grave and weep,
> I am not there, I do not sleep.
> I am the thousand winds that blow,

I am the diamond glints of snow.
I am the sunlight on ripened grain,
I am the gentle autumn's rain.

When you awaken in the morning's hush,
I am the quick, uplifting thrush
Of quiet birds in circled flight.
I am the soft stars that shine at night.
Do not stand by my grave and cry.
I am not there, I did not die.

Well-considered Sacrifice

A newspaper columnist is privileged to meet many wonderful people. Some are famous, some are not. Let me tell you about a wonderful person I met recently.

Because she is an elderly woman and because of circumstances in the story, I cannot give her name or address. That might compromise her safety.

About two months ago, the elderly woman, a stranger to me, called the Onlooker, saying, "I have read your column for a long time, and I'm wondering if you can help me with a problem.

"Recently, I found a large amount of money while I was out shopping. I have tried hard to find the owner. I even put an ad in the newspaper, but I have been unsuccessful. I didn't dare tell the amount, location or the kind of container it was in, because that would have given it away, and anyone could have claimed it.

"Most of my friends tell me I should just keep the money now, because I truly could use it. I'm not very well off. But, I keep thinking the money might belong to some other elderly person who needs it more than I do. Can you suggest anything?"

So, I wrote an Onlooker item telling of her plight. We received many calls from people who had lost money recently, but none matched the circumstances in this case. After a month had passed, I called my elderly friend and told her that she could now spend the money with a clear conscience. We had tried very hard to find the owner.

This was her response:

"Well, Mr. Hough, I think you are right. My conscience is clear enough. But, I have been thinking about it a lot, and I know of a couple of elderly people who are worse off than I am.

"I think I'll give each of them half of the money. They have a problem paying their bills, and the money could brighten their lives at Christmas. I'll make it all right on my own. They need it more."

Sacrifice like that should make any of us much humbler. I'm putting that great lady at the top of my favorite-readers list.

Barney Doesn't Bark

Barney, the car-horn-sounding mongrel dog owned by Mrs. Eileen Corr, DeWitt Township treasurer, created more chaos this week.

Readers may have read about Barney in an earlier Onlooker column, which noted that he is impatient when left alone in the car. He sits up in the driver's seat and leans his paw on the car horn button. On many occasions, he has embarrassed Mrs. Corr.

Clinton County Sheriff's Detective Richard May told me that Barney created some real havoc earlier this week, when Mrs. Corr came upon an accident on U.S. 27 near DeWitt. There was great confusion at the scene. Traffic was down to one lane as Mrs. Corr and Barney drove by.

Suddenly, Mrs. Corr saw her daughter's car at the accident scene. She quickly pulled her car to the roadside and went to investigate. She found her daughter in the backseat of the police car. As she talked with her daughter and as several other police patrols tried to sort out the traffic mess, old Barney was back there sounding the car horn.

"As if there wasn't enough confusion around there, Barney had to do his thing," said Officer May. "Officers kept saying: 'Why in blankety-blank is that damned guy over there blowing his horn?' Mrs. Corr went to scold Barney, and he stopped for a minute. Then, he was right back at it. By the way, Jim, I learned that Barney is a left-handed dog."

No, Dick, you mean that Barney is left-pawed. Dogs don't have hands. Any policeman ought to know that.

Black Angel

Racial prejudice is slowly ending in American society. As some people kick away the prejudice in their minds, they wonder how it ever got there in the first place. The following letter to the Onlooker offers a perfect case in point:

Dear Mr. Hough,

When you read this, you will know why I wish my name kept anonymous. I had to tell someone about the beautiful experience I had recently.

I am a white female in my early fifties. I have multiple sclerosis, and many terrible things have happened to my family lately.

One day recently, I broke completely and was ready to end it all, but someone persisted in knocking at my door. When I finally went to see who it was, I pulled back the curtain to see a black man. As I live near one of the ladies who was murdered recently, I have been very careful not to let anyone in or leave my door unlocked. But, when I saw the man this day, I was so despondent that I thought it might be the one who was killing women. So, I opened the door to him, hoping he would do the job for me.

Instead, he saw how distraught I was. He stayed with me and held me, to keep me from harming myself. The phone rang, and it was my sister. He answered the phone. I know how this must have upset her to hear a man answer. When he told her the state I was in, she said she would be right over...

I know there isn't room in your column to print all of this, but I want you to know that the man was Roosevelt Webb. He is a meter reader for the Board of Water and Light. This dear man stayed with me until my sister got here and for a long time after. He refused to leave until I would look him in the eye and promise him I would be OK. He cried with me.

When my sister walked in and saw him standing over me, with his cheek on my prickly curlers and his arms wrapped around me, she said it was the most beautiful thing she had ever seen. My sister had a black orchid in an artificial bouquet when she came in. I feel it was very significant. I will never again be afraid of a black man.

I hope someday I will be led to write this whole story and tell why I was hurting badly enough to want to take my own life and how this total stranger came in and saved my life. It might not have been so significant if he had not been black, because the reason I opened the door to him was an evil reason. It turned out that he was a black angel.

While the writer of the above letter learned a racial lesson that day, it was all a matter of routine for Roosevelt Webb. He has been a Board of Water and Light employee for six years and has often demonstrated his compassion. Dennis Casteele, BWL spokesman, said stories of Webb's kind acts are heard often.

When I asked Webb's permission to publish the woman's letter, his answer said it all: "Do whatever you like, Jim. I'd be proud to be mentioned in your column, but I'm sure you know that neighborliness has nothing to do with color."

Indeed, it does not.

Making a Difference

Perhaps it's time that I confessed that I have been lying to readers of this column.

That lie comes each time I give the impression that all calls and letters to the Onlooker are of a happy and upbeat nature. It's time I told you that this is not true.

A large portion of the reader calls and letters tell of personal tragedy, heartache and shattered lives. On many days, I feel more like a social worker than a columnist. Those kind of stories don't make the Onlooker, of course, because publishing them would invade privacy or violate the spirit of the column. For the most part, we'd like to keep this column upbeat. There's enough personal trauma elsewhere.

But there are a lot of folks living shattered lives. Many of them call to ask advice or just to talk. I'm down-in-the-mouth on many days when I leave this desk.

So, knowing all of that, you can understand why I was so pleased to read a letter telling of a happy turnabout in one of those troubled lives. I am withholding the name, of course, but the letter reads as follows:

Dear Mr. Hough,

Many years ago, I was extremely depressed. Life seemed hopeless and evidence of evil acts overwhelmed me. Living from day to day was a struggle. I could see no evidence of a loving God at work.

One day, I read in the State Journal an account to two teen-age girls who were murdered and dumped in a park near Bath. I kept asking myself: Why is life like this? I didn't know how to vent the feelings of outrage, frustration and hopelessness that I felt.

So, I sat down and wrote a letter to a total stranger, a newspaper writer who wrote not of violence, child abuse, rape and murder, but rather of giant cucumbers and radishes, and of man's humanity, rather than inhumanity.

That newspaper writer was, of course, you, Mr. Hough. A day or two later, you called me and we talked. I remember part of it was about the Vietnam War, because I had mentioned something about that also.

Time passed, my depression grew worse. My marriage of twenty years ended in divorce. I drank heavily, smoked marijuana and took tranquilizers. I wanted to die, but I didn't want to commit suicide. I ended up at the alcoholic treatment program at St. Lawrence Hospital and from there to the fellowship of Alcoholics Anonymous. My personal hell began to subside.

Many times during those years, I thought of you and that phone call. Something about the fact that you took time out from your life gave me a small measure of assurance that life is really worth living and that there really is a spark of love somewhere. So, thank you, Mr. Hough, for taking a few minutes of your day for me.

It's been almost two years since I left the treatment facility at St. Lawrence. In that time, I have not taken one tranquilizer, one drink of alcohol or one puff of marijuana. I do this with the help of A.A. My life has improved. I do not feel hopeless. Today, I want to live.

The Onlooker congratulates St. Lawrence Hospital and Alcoholics Anonymous. This is just one little example of their great work.

Fecund Fly Facts

Would you believe that the Michigan Department of Agriculture raises about forty thousand houseflies per week at a Michigan State University laboratory?

It's true. And, not only that, the flies have a pedigree. They belong to a strain that goes back to 1938, before the days of DDT. About one thousand generations of the flies have been raised since then. Michigan has been in the fly-raising business since 1963. We borrowed a few flies from the Federal Food and Drug Administration to get started.

OK, reader, now that we have your attention, we will answer your question: What on Earth do they do with flies?

This is no fly-by-night operation. They raise flies in the daytime, too. John Calkins, Michigan Department of Agriculture information director, explains that the flies are used to test for pesticide content in foods.

It's quite simple. You put some of the super-sensitive flies in a flask with the food sample. If the food has pesticides in it, the super-sensitive flies keel over dead. That's why it is so important that the flies have the pedigree and no hint of pesticide immunity in their ancestry.

Actually, when the fly goes dead — kerplop in the flask — that is not really the end of the test. It is only a signal for the lab boys to make more definitive tests of the food. By the way, not much pesticide is found in Michigan foods.

A housefly lives about ten days after it reaches the adult stage. However, flies are used in the food test when they are one day old. So, if they get through that first day without going dead, kerplop, they can live to a ripe old age of ten days. They get a dandy diet of reconstituted, evaporated milk.

The lab is kept at an even temperature of eighty degrees, which flies seem to prefer. The eggs of a fly hatch in about twenty-four hours and become maggots in three days. After a week of feeding on horsemeat and alfalfa, the maggots go into the shell stage. Three days later, the adult fly is buzzing about.

Doesn't that completely overwhelm you? Zowie! Onlooker readers are not used to such scientific treats.

The Chase Is Over

I sat on a log in front of my cabin on the shore of Lake Superior a couple of weeks ago. It was a peaceful moment — the swish of the waves, the call of the seagulls, the whir of the wind in the pines.

Then, I looked up to see my old Labrador, Candy, stumbling toward me. She made it to my side, lay down in the sand and put her head on my foot. I reached down to stroke her head.

Suddenly, the moment was no longer peaceful. A seagull came close. Candy only growled a little. Any other time she'd have jumped up and chased the gull — a game she loved on that shore for thirteen years. But, the chase is over for her. Those old hips hurt her now when she runs. I looked at those aging, gray whiskers. My tears came. This would be Candy's last summer at the cabin.

Petting her head, I remembered so many great times we had had together. She's the best darned dog a man could want. She has been smart, perfectly behaved and so loyal to the family.

When I proposed to my wife twenty-eight years ago, I said I'd give her a ring if she'd let me have a dog. A couple of weeks after the honeymoon, I came home with a tiny beagle puppy, Scoopy. He was a great hunting companion and friend for sixteen years. He was spoiled rotten, even slept on the foot of my bed.

When Scoopy came to the end, I thought I'd never get another dog. Too much pain out at the end, I said. But, my boy Steve was twelve. He cried when I told him he could not get a dog to replace Scoopy.

After stern lectures from my mom, I caved in to the pressure. Steve said he wanted a black Labrador. I heard about Candy, a dropout from the Leader Dog School for the Blind. They said she was too shy. They had to flunk her.

I'll never forget the day I brought her home. We parked in the driveway and waited for Steve to come to the car. He looked at the dog on my lap, then at me and then the tears came. Happy tears. Steve had his dog.

Within minutes, he had her trained to do tricks. It was love at first sight. I swear you could teach a Lab to play euchre. They are so smart and so gentle that the leader dog school now has gone to them exclusively.

But, Steve grew up, graduated from high school and went off to school in Denver for two years. Candy became my dog. I loved every minute of it. She's pretty special.

Labor Day in Lansing was cold and rainy. I looked up to see Candy sitting in front of the fireplace and staring hard at me.

"Build a fire for me, Jim," she was saying. It was a message I had got from her hundreds of times. Those aching hips needed some warmth. I built a fire. She curled up in front of it. Who knows, maybe she can last the winter, I thought. But I could not bear to see her in pain for very long.

I'll never forget that day when we had to put Scoopy to sleep. Tears flowed down the face of my dear veterinarian friend, Dr. F.O. Grounds, as he prepared the needle. He and Scoopy were friends, too.

Clearing his throat, Doc said, "Jim, what's important now is to remember all of the good things that Scoopy brought into your life while he was here with you. Don't dwell on what he takes out of your life as he leaves."

Yeah, I know, Doc. Those are good and true words. But, oh, how it hurts.

Tears for a Friend

"I'll marry you if you'll let me keep a rabbit-hunting hound in the house," I told my wife Darl as we sat on the bank of the Chippewa River in Mt. Pleasant sixteen years ago.

She accepted the proposal, but she thought I was kidding about the dog. A few weeks after our honeymoon, I came home with a tiny, beautiful beagle puppy. He was so small and cuddly that he fit into my overcoat pocket. I named him Scoopy. Within minutes, he won my wife's heart.

Scoopy grew up to be quite a character. Because I think his story and his effect upon the lives of me and my family may be typical of that experienced by thousands of other dog owners, I'm writing about him here.

When he was only six months old, Scoopy howled his objection as I quit throwing a rubber ball, which he liked to retrieve, and I began to assemble a Christmas tree stand. The dog sat with cocked ears, watching me put up the tree. I stood back, admired the tree and wound up like Mickey Lolich, to throw a handful of tinsel on the tree. My wife screamed as Scoopy howled and leaped at the tree. The whole thing came crashing down. Scoopy thought I had thrown his ball.

Then there was the time my wife lost her watch. We found it two years later. Scoopy had buried it in a large living room flower pot.

Scoopy nearly met death many times. Once, we were driving about sixty miles an hour down a highway near Alma, when a pheasant flew across the road in front of our car. Scoopy saw it, howled and jumped out of the car window. He struck the roadway, rolled, tumbled and skidded a long way.

I quickly backed up the car. I expected to find my dog dead. Instead, there he sat, shivering with fright and licking some bare spots where the hair was torn off. Wow! No limbs were broken. He was quick to learn, though, and he never pulled that stunt again.

Scoopy, a registered beagle and son of ex-field champions, was a fantastic hunter. He had a howl that could be heard several counties away. I could tell stories all day about our hunting experiences together.

Probably the best example came one day when Scoopy and I took a friend hunting. The friend, Harold Janiszewski, a state police trooper, suggested we try a swamp in northwestern Isabella County, where there were a few snowshoe rabbits.

Sure enough, Scoopy found one. He howled and ran through deep snow in pursuit of the big snowshoe rabbit. I was the first to get a shot at the rabbit, and I missed. "Ski" shot twice at it the next time it circled. He missed. The dog kept going. On the third time around, "Ski" finally got the rabbit.

Scoopy, only about thirty feet behind the rabbit, roared to the scene, skidded to a halt, looked down at the dead rabbit, and then pointed his nose high in the air to let out his loudest howl ever. Then Scoopy flopped to the earth in exhaustion. He seemed to be saying, "Holy Shazam, you guys, it's about time you got 'im. I'm bushed."

Scoopy's rabbit-chasing once got me into a whole lot of trouble at Mt. Pleasant. We lived in a house about a block from the hospital. Each night, before going to bed, I'd let Scoopy out the front door for a last visit to the maple tree in the front yard.

One winter night, Scoopy was leaning on that maple tree when a rabbit hopped by. Suddenly, Scoopy saw the rabbit, and he let out a loud, mournful howl. The chase was on.

I ran after the dog, leaping over fences and dashing around garages. I could see lights coming on in homes along the dog's route. Three times, that rabbit circled the hospital. Three times, mind you. Somebody called the police to complain about the noise. An officer arrived. "What the hell is going on, Jim?" he asked.

"Just shoot the rabbit," I pleaded with the officer.

"Naw, that'd only make more noise," he said. Finally, nearly at the point of exhaustion, I caught Scoopy. The officer didn't arrest me because he had a rabbit-hunting dog of his own, and he understood.

Yes, Scoopy was a great hunter. But he was something else, too — a great friend and companion. I'd come home from work and flop down on the davenport, feeling kind of weary. Scoopy would jump up there, lie down beside me and nudge his nose under my hand. I'd scratch his ears and, suddenly, there was tranquility. The world was right again.

But, Scoopy grew old, very old. He was sixteen this year. He could no longer walk. His arthritic pain was great. His doctor, F.O. Grounds, finally found the courage to say, "I can do no more for him, Jim. It's time now to end his pain."

Scoopy is sleeping now...and I don't care who sees my tears.

Pint-size Spirit

Pride in my children has possessed me, and I just have to tell you about it. If my copy is slightly stained with tears of joy, perhaps you will understand.

Our daughter Linda, six, and son Steve, four, announced several days ago that they wanted to give one of their toys to someone who would not have toys at Christmas.

They told us, "It doesn't count unless you give up something you really like."

Linda gave her doll buggy. Steve gave his tank. Both items were last year's Christmas gifts.

As the toys were taken from the house, Linda and Steve beamed, but Dad's eyes were wet. He had a big lump in his throat. Boy, how the youngsters can show up the adults when it comes to displaying the Christmas spirit.

Backward Up There?

Paradise, a tiny Upper Peninsula community on Lake Superior's Whitefish Bay, is far, far behind the times. It lacks many of the things we find in abundance here in Lansing.

Take pollution, for instance. Lansing, and all big cities, have a lot of that. But, Paradise has little. What Lansingite would dare to make snow ice cream with snow in his front yard? It's easy in Paradise. That beautiful whiteness. It's everywhere. It's a clean serenity. And, if you are a city slicker who has never tasted snow ice cream, well...you have missed a lot.

(In case you get the chance to make it, the recipe for snow ice cream is: One cup of condensed milk, one cup of sugar, two raw eggs and one teaspoon of vanilla. Stir well. Gradually add freshly fallen snow and continue stirring until thick like ice cream. Don't use Lansing's snow. Wait until you are in the snowy north.)

Paradise is behind the times in other ways, too. On Christmas Day, Mr. and Mrs. Albert Gillingham prepared a special tray of Christmas-dinner goodies, which they took to the remote cabin of Jack LaLone, a bachelor. You can see how Paradise is behind the times. Folks there don't know of their need for Community Chests, Salvation Armies, Volunteers of America and all of the other social service agencies. Folks in Paradise think problems can be solved without such agencies. They think the solution lies in simple neighborliness. Imagine that! Paradise is sure behind the times.

"Spence," operator of a bar and restaurant, heard that a neighbor down the street wanted to keep his restaurant open this winter. So, "Spence" helped by closing the restaurant portion of his own business. His explanation was simple: "Aw, it will be a long winter, and we will all need to share a little to get along." Imagine that! A businessman willing to share a little with a competitor? Wow! Paradise is sure behind the times.

Paradise doesn't have a licensed barber. But, a lot of folks drop in every couple of weeks to visit Lionel Fairchild, and they come out looking clean-cut. No money changes hands, but Lionel has never had to ask twice for a favor in that behind-the-times community.

Paradise has a few criminals, but everyone knows who they are, and so does the county sheriff. So, the criminals don't pull off much crime. Paradise is behind the times in law enforcement, too. It has no police department.

Fran Monk whips his snowplow out of the garage any hour of the day or night that a storm hits, and he renders a lifeline service to many remote areas. Paradise doesn't have a public works department or any similar city hall divisions common to cities.

To encourage winter tourism, some Paradise folks went out and marked snowmobile trails in wooded and remote state land. It worked, too. And Paradise doesn't even have a Greater Paradise Chamber of Commerce. Imagine that!

I could write on and on about the quality of life in Paradise. There are so many other ways in which those folks are behind the times.

But, what I really want to do is apologize to Paradise folks for the noise pollution our family brought there last week, during our annual mid-winter trek to our rustic cabin.

Until we got there, the only noises heard around the cabin were the creak of timbers as the wind struck the cabin and the whine of the wind in the pine trees.

Then our family added noise pollution: The crunching of our snowshoes as we disturbed the freshly fallen snow; the crackling of the wood fire in the Franklin stove; the occasional crack of the new .22 rifle I gave Steve for Christmas; the sound of my wife yelling into the wind to call the children in to dinner when they didn't want to come.

The squeals of delight that came from our daughter as she watched her dad take a backward flip off a snow saucer as it whizzed down a hill. "You look real good in midair, Dad," she giggled. And there was that eternal, loud snoring of our fourteen-year-old beagle Scoopy, as he sprawled on the rug in front of the stove.

Yes, I guess we were pretty noisy in that quiet community last week. I hope the folks of Paradise didn't mind too much.

Modern-day Hero

Will Rogers once said: "We can't all be heroes because some of us have to sit on the curb to clap as they go by."

A long-time friend of mine, Bill Anderson of the Grand Ole Opry, wrote a song a few years ago, when he became discouraged at the preponderance of highly paid spoiled brats in the world of sports. The song title asked a question: "Where Have All the Heroes Gone?"

That question surely nags us all today and not only when we think of sports. We wonder where have all the heroes gone when we look at politics, religion and so many other important areas where dishonesty is uncovered and reported daily.

But, readers, take heart. I search a bit harder than most for the optimistic side. I wrote Bill Anderson recently to tell him that one hero is still alive and well — not wearing a white hat and riding his white horse into the sunset, but broadcasting Detroit Tiger baseball games.

That hero is George Kell. I'm not a sports columnist, and this is not a sports column. But George Kell can qualify as anybody's hero.

Recently, I visited with Kell when he was honored at a big shindig in Lansing. As most know, George is the greatest third baseman in Detroit Tiger history and maybe in the history of the American League. This summer, he received the greatest honor that can come to a baseball player. He was inducted to the Hall of Fame.

I asked George what that meant to him, and he replied this way: "Jim, I have tried to answer that question for reporters for weeks now. It seems each time I do, it is never enough. There seems no way I can truly describe how grateful I am."

What was the first thing you did when you learned of the honor, I asked him.

"I flew home to Swifton, Arkansas, to take the news to my father, who lies there in a nursing home. It was my father's dream that his three sons would make the major leagues. Two of us did. The third never got the chance, because he was killed in the war.

"When I gave the news of my acceptance to the Hall of Fame to my father there in the nursing home, I watched tears flow down his face. That might have been my biggest thrill in baseball," Kell said.

I know there are a lot of great athletes whom some call heroes today. But it seems to me that the only real heroes are those who demonstrate leadership, compassion and love off the field.

Yes, Bill Anderson, one hero is still around. The induction of

George Kell to baseball's Hall of Fame put tears on the face of his father. It also put happy tears on the faces of thousands — not to mention a giant lump in the throat of this writer.

The incredible fielding plays and hitting of George Kell brought him endless standing ovations throughout his fifteen-year career. The amazing thing is, though, that it was not all of those great baseball statistics and plays that caused the flow of happy tears on the faces of his father and his fans. No, those tears were caused by the admiration felt for Kell off the field. Take note, young athletes, that's where real heroes are made — off the field.

As Ed Howe once said, "A boy doesn't have to go to war to be a hero. He can say he doesn't like pie when he sees there isn't enough to go around."

They Hear Harwell

The four hundred youngsters in the Civic Center audience at the Little League baseball awards dinner this week were restless — just like all kids at any banquet. Several speakers, including Tiger Manager Sparky Anderson, had been to the podium.

Suddenly, there was silence. The kids turned to the stage and listened with rapt attention. Ernie Harwell, Tiger broadcaster, was speaking. It was a voice they knew. They hung on every word, as Ernie told them this story:

"All of you young baseball players are lucky. So many people — parents, coaches and others — are reaching out to you every day, helping you along life's path.

"A great poet, Robert Browning, once wrote: 'A man's reach should exceed his grasp or what is Heaven for?' Willie Mays, the great center-fielder for the Giants, had such a reach.

"A man once came to Willie to ask a favor. He told Willie that he knew of a young man who admired Mays, but who was leading a bad life and about to get into deep trouble with the law. The man asked Willie to go and talk to the boy.

"Willie did that. He told the boy he ought to quit running with a bad crowd, and that he'd better change the direction of his life.

"It worked. That boy's admiration for Willie caused him to take Willie's advice. He changed his life and later became a very successful man. I'd like to tell you that he grew up to replace his hero in center field — his long-time dream — but it didn't happen. That young man was O.J. Simpson.

"Yes, Willie's reach exceeded his grasp. I urge you young people to listen hard to your parents and coaches. You'll become better baseball players, but, more importantly, you'll feel happiness and success creeping into your lives."

As Ernie finished, hundreds of small hands created the loudest applause of the night. Nobody communicates with youngsters better than Ernie Harwell. Personally, I've never met a nicer man.

Nature's Lessons

Getting to my Upper Peninsula cabin is quite a task, even on a warm summer day. Getting there in winter is...well...it's something else.

But, my family thinks getting there is important. My wife Darl, as hardy a female as any columnist ever married, and my children, Linda, ten, and Steve, eight, think as I do: Anyone who lets a little weather scare him misses a lot of life.

It was in that spirit that we headed north a week ago. But before we reached the Big Mac bridge, I was close to burying that hardy-northwoods-philosophy stuff for the security of civilization.

About twenty miles south of the bridge, we ran into what folks there said was the worst blizzard in years. I could write chapters about that awful, blinding blow of white and about the fear it brought to us on the lonely freeway. I could write chapters about the fifty people who spent the night in the Mackinaw City Presbyterian Church, after they could not find motel space.

But, the best part was how we shared peanut butter sandwiches with a young couple and their children from Ontonagon, at a motel that was truly cut off from all other life for a few hours that night. That special warmth, that binding-together quality fills all people in a time of common need.

It's a beautiful thing. It reminded me of how warm and considerate big-city folks became in Lansing, during the blizzard of 1967. It takes something like that now and then to renew your faith in humanity. Yes, sir, a good old blizzard is hard to beat.

But, our winter vacation brought an even richer experience. A day after the big, white blow, we reached the vicinity of our cabin on Lake Superior. I say the vicinity because that's the only word that fits. When you are standing in my cabin, the nearest plowed road is more than a half-mile away. We all wore snowshoes and crunched our way down a wooded trail.

The beauty and solitude of that trail take your breath away — the snow-covered pines, the four-foot drifts that bring a gentle, graceful architecture to the land.

Linda is the poet in our family. She stopped for a rest and said, ''Gee, Dad. Look at those beautiful pine trees. They look like they are trimmed in white lace.'' I couldn't add to that.

At one point on the walk in, Steve lagged behind a little. His short legs were just learning the rhythm of walking on snowshoes. I was pretty bushed, too. Old Dad had to pull the toboggan loaded with a duffel bag of clothes and the box filled with a week's supply of groceries.

So, Steve and I rested. We sat on the duffel bag. I answered a flood of questions about a rabbit track, and then I saw Steve looking up at me with an expression that I could not read. "What's wrong, son?" I asked.

"Oh, I wuz jess looking at how happy you are, Dad," he said.

That boy has the darndest way of choking me up sometimes. I put my arm around his small shoulders and muttered something about how boys like him help make dads happy. I didn't even wipe the happy tears away. Just let 'em freeze there for good, I thought. Emotional moments like that between a man and his son should be preserved forever.

Later that night, the children were snug in their sleeping bags. The cabin was toasty warm. The wind howled outside. My wife was buried in a good book. I sat in front of the wood stove, enjoying the quiet of the crackling fire.

I had no thoughts. That's what made it beautiful. No clacking of typewriters, no TV plots to tolerate. Just peace. Somehow, I had the feeling that I could settle the Vietnam War, if I just could get the world leaders to my cabin on a bright, wintry day.

I have to confess, though, that one date did pop into my mind a few times up there. It was February 22. That's when the Detroit Tigers open spring training at Lakeland, Florida. And, whenever I think of baseball, I think of Charlie Hass, State Journal assistant sports editor.

Charlie, undoubtedly, would have described the scene this way: "The northwoods were as quiet as Ray Oyler's bat, and the world would boast a lot fewer psychiatric couches if more people could spend a vacation there."

A Day at the Races

The best part of my vacation was not the peaceful splash of Lake Superior's waves in front of my cabin.

The best part of my vacation was not the heavy catches of nice perch in Whitefish Bay.

The best part of my vacation was not the beautiful weather, which made swimming a daily event.

The best part of my vacation was not the boat rides up the beautiful Tahquamenon River.

It was the frog races. Yeah, frog races...right there on the shores of Gitche Gumee. Boy, if only I was a sports writer. Could I ever write a story about a frog-racing tournament.

The races began when my children, Linda, eleven, and Steve, ten, found a frog-filled pond near the big lake. They led their friends, Wayne and Bruce Mills, of Brimley, and Martha and Nancy Tooley, of Mt. Pleasant, to the pond. After each had caught a frog, the children lined off a frog-racing course.

The frogs were given such unlikely names as Fast Freddie, Froggy, Hoppy, Jasper, Sam, Croaky and Peeper. The start was tense, as each frog approached the starting point. Then the squeals of the children could be heard far out on Lake Superior: "Go, Jasper!" "Hop, Hoppy!" "Come on, Freddie!"

Wayne Mills sat back confidently because his frog, Jasper, was twice the size of the others. But, lunker Jasper was sluggish and never made it off the starting line. Nancy's frog, Fast Freddie, won easily.

Wayne talked Nancy into trading Jasper for Freddie before the second race began. But, Wayne outsmarted himself because Jasper won the second race with one great leap.

I asked the kids if I could enter a frog in the race. "What would you call him?" one of them asked. I said I'd call him Spiro or Milhouse or Horatio. They held a vote and said I could not enter because I am an adult and frog racing is just for kids.

I was darned sorry that I was not a kid. It looked like great fun.

Later in the day, there was a great tragedy. A snake came along and ate one of the frogs. Nobody seemed to know which frog it was, although I suspect it was Fast Freddie.

Linda and Steve are considering the formation of a Frog Racing Association, with an annual tournament on the shores of Gitche

Gumee. They think they can interest Paradise businesses in the venture and sell tickets to spectators.

I'd sure buy a ticket. Frog racing is as exciting as baseball, and Fast Freddie was as fierce a competitor as Dick McAuliffe — until the snake got 'im.

Why is frog racing just for kids? How come kids have all the fun?

Meeting the Past

Mrs. Patricia Ann Spicer, of Grand Ledge, and Mrs. Betty Misener, of Lansing, became close friends during the past three months, because they are both parishioners at the Grand Ledge Nazarene Church.

They were talking about Pat's five children recently, as Betty worked in the church nursery. Betty asked Pat if she had parents living in this area, and Pat explained that she was blessed with two families.

"I was adopted when I was only a year old," Pat told Betty, "so I had my adopted parents for the last thirty years, and I recently found my real father. I never have found my mother, though."

Betty continued the casual conversation, asking the name of Pat's real father. "His name is Fred Hyatt, of Lansing," Pat said. She heard a gasp from Betty and then was shocked to see Betty collapse in a faint. She had suffered a heart attack.

Later, when Betty began to recover at St. Lawrence Hospital, the facts unfolded.

Betty is Pat's mother. They had searched for each other for the past twenty years. Betty is still at St. Lawrence Hospital, recovering from her shock and her heart attack.

"It was a Christmas miracle," Betty told the Onlooker. "Pat is thirty-one years old now. When I was divorced thirty years ago, I lost her to an adoption agency. I never thought I'd ever see her again, even though I have searched for her for years.

"The people who adopted her and raised her, Mr. and Mr. Robert Wilson, of Lansing, have done a fabulous job. Pat is a great lady today. Yes, it's truly a miracle," Betty said.

However, Pat said, that "moment of revelation" was a frightening thing. "She kept saying I was her daughter, and I couldn't figure it out. Doctors said her heart simply stopped. I was really scared. What an amazing thing that a mother and daughter should meet that way after thirty years," Pat said.

"We hope for better things for Mom in the future," Pat continued. "She is a real sweet lady, and I love her very, very much. She is so proud of my children — her five grandchildren, whom she didn't even know she had. This is truly a great Christmas for all of us," Pat said.

One More Reprieve

As you read this, I'll probably be sitting close to the Franklin stove in my cabin on the frozen shore of Lake Superior.

Paradise is more than Paradise in name. It is once more a real paradise for me, as I spend another Christmas with my family, Linda, Steve, and wife Darl, at our cabin.

I really thought last year would end our tradition of Christmas at the cabin. After all, Linda is now a college freshman (shouldn't it be freshwoman?), and Steve is a high school junior. Surely, Darl and I thought, they won't want to leave their boyfriends and girlfriends to make that trip to the quiet north with their parents again.

But, we were wrong. Linda and Steve demanded that we head north again this year, and they began to talk excitedly about snowshoe walks in the woods, ice skating on Lake Superior's inlet ponds, cutting firewood, winter walks to the Tahquamenon Falls, toboggan rides, cutting a Christmas tree from their own property behind the cabin.

I told the family that I had not planned for a trip to the cabin this Christmas, and Linda responded: "Well, Dad, you'd better get planning, or else we might leave you home when we go again this year."

I got to planning right away. I wouldn't miss that family fun for anything. So, another year and another Christmas at the cabin.

Now the question is: What about next year? Will Linda and Steve want to go up north again? I'm betting they will. But, I also know that there will come a time soon when we can't repeat that wonderful family tradition.

Still, there may be a ray of hope for the future. Someday, Linda and Steve will have kids of their own to take up there for a Paradise Christmas. Maybe, just maybe, they'll invite Grandma and Grandpa.

Grandpa? Good grief, I'm a long, long way from being one of those...aren't I? Hmmmm, I wonder if a grandpa would enjoy cutting firewood, walking on snowshoes, ice skating...? I bet he would. Life in Paradise is great at any age.

Rewards of Winter

The first thing I did was take a bath when I returned from Paradise, after a week-long vacation in the frozen north. I wanted to get all of that black off me from hugging my Franklin stove so tightly all week.

The temperature dropped to twenty-five degrees below zero, or lower, three days in a row, and the National Weather Service office at Sault Sainte Marie said there were many colder "pockets," where the mercury dipped to forty below during those three days. The "high" temperature in Paradise one day last week was five degrees below zero.

And the snow...my, oh my, the snow. The weather service reported that more than one hundred and fifty inches of snow had fallen in Paradise so far this year. Drifts have nearly buried my cabin. Driving through Paradise is like driving through a long, white tunnel. Good grief, where will they put all of the snow that is still to come this winter?

However, while the air freezes noses and the snow creates backaches, the winter spectacle is great for the eyes and the brain.

On that day when the temperature reached a high of only five below zero, my daughter, Linda, said: "Hey, Dad, let's bundle up and take a walk at the Tahquamenon Falls. The sun is bright, and it will be a great day to get pictures."

Linda doesn't give up easily, and she soon had Darl, my wife, and me bundled up like teddy bears and headed to the car. We drove to the area and walked in to view the Upper Falls.

Surely, it was the most spectacular winter sight I've ever seen. The trees wore a beautiful white lace, and those giant columns of ice at the falls were glistening in so many hues — bright blue, orange, red, rust.

We weren't alone as we stood there, staring in disbelief at that winter spectacle. There was a large crowd of winter visitors to the falls. It was truly exciting to hear the "oohs," "ahhs" and "wows" coming from the spectators.

Yes, it gets cold in Michigan's northland, but the rewards of winter splendor are great.

The Simple Things

Just returned from the best vacation in years, in Nashville, Tennessee, where we were guests of Bill and Becky Anderson.

Strangely, it was not the glitter of Nashville's music stars and Saturday night in the performers' lounge backstage at the Grand Ole Opry that dazzled me. Sure, it was fun to visit with those famous people, but there is no substitute for good friendship. So, the things I'll remember most about that vacation will be:

Playing baseball in Bill's yard with his son, Jamey.

Saturday afternoon sitting in Bill's spacious home and hearing him say, "Are you having a good time, Jim? Is there anything you miss back in Michigan?"

I told him I missed the Tigers, and that I'd be watching them on TV if I was back in Michigan. Bill, an even bigger baseball nut than I am, turned to the controls for his TV satellite dish and instantly had the Tiger game on TV.

What an afternoon. We watched every pitch as the Tigers whipped the White Sox. A visit with Dolly Parton couldn't match that.

Bill and Becky invited us to join them at Easter services at a Methodist church. "Jan's going to sing there, and I wouldn't miss it for anything," Bill said.

Jan Howard, a longtime Grand Ole Opry star and a former member of Bill's band, has suffered through a world of tragedy. Her son was killed in Vietnam and another son committed suicide on the first anniversary of his brother's death. Later, Jan lost her husband to an illness. She had stood for those funerals in that church. It took great courage for her to stand there to sing on Easter.

Jan has been a longtime friend, and I found myself wiping away tears as she sang "How Great Thou Art." So beautiful. Embarrassed, I reached for my handkerchief. I turned to see Bill reaching for his, too. Fact is, there wasn't a dry eye in the place.

And I'll remember knocking about the Nashville area with Bill in his big, white Lincoln as we searched for bargains in outlet stores of western boot factories.

"I bought a pair real cheap," Bill said, proudly pointing to a new pair of boots. "They're seconds. There's a slight flaw there. Heck, they'll never spot it in the front row. I'll wear 'em to perform at the Opry tonight." He did, too.

I won't forget my visit with Roy Acuff at his Opry dressing room. He's an American institution. He's eighty this year and has been performing at the Grand Ole Opry for forty-eight years. He's performed at the White House for every president in the past twenty years. I asked him how he was feeling at eighty.

"Not well, Jim," he confessed. "I have circulatory problems and my legs hurt me after a show. The doctors told me years ago that I'd be in a wheelchair before I was seventy. I'll keep going as long as I can. We don't want any wheelchairs carrying Roy Acuff to the Grand Ole Opry stage, do we?"

We don't, indeed.

And I wish I had thought to get the name of the Lansing man and his family who introduced themselves to me at the hotel where we stayed.

The man came to me in the lobby and said, "You're Jim Hough, aren't you? We're from Lansing and we read your column. You'll never believe it. I said to my wife a few minutes ago that I couldn't wait to get back to Lansing, so I could call Jim Hough and tell him I had seen Bill Anderson and gotten his autograph in Nashville. And then I looked up to see you standing right here in Nashville."

I wish you could have seen the shock come over the man's face as Anderson stepped to my side and introduced his friend, Jim Hough. Like a dummy, I neglected to get the Lansing man's name. Perhaps he'll call me so we can compare notes on our Nashville vacations.

Although the Andersons often invite us to visit them, we are hesitant, for fear we might be imposing on them. After all, Bill is performing on two TV shows and producing another on the Nashville Network, doing road tours and is now the owner of more than one hundred Po Folks Restaurants. But, as we parted last week in Nashville, Darl and I saw Bill wipe tears from his face.

"Excuse the emotion," he said, "but the more successful a person becomes, the more he realizes the importance of real friendship. Hurry back, Becky and I will miss you."

I won't forget that moment either.

The Loneliest Time

"It's only a question of time before a drunken driver causes pain in your life."

That's a quote I've heard so many, many times from my friends in law enforcement that it never really registered. We always think of those things as happening to strangers.

On Saturday night, a drunken driver lost control of his car in Nashville, Tennessee. The vehicle crossed the highway median and struck the car of an innocent driver head-on. Suddenly, a drunken driver had put pain in my life. The innocent victim was Becky Anderson, a wonderful lady and wife of my close friend, Bill Anderson, of the Grand Ole Opry.

Becky, alone in the car, suffered severe brain injuries. She has been in critical condition at Nashville's General Hospital. It has been a nightmare for Bill and their six-year-old son Jamey.

I talked to Bill yesterday. When he heard my voice, he broke into tears. After a moment, he said, "I'm sorry, Jim. I've been courageous until this moment. I guess you are special, and I know how much Becky means to you and Darl. It's a terrible thing to look at a loved one and ponder the consequences of brain injuries.

"But, I'm feeling a tiny bit better today. Until last night, Becky had not responded. I held her hand, and I told her to squeeze my hand if she knew I was there. She did. It was an important moment for us all. This morning, a doctor asked her name. It was a weak reply, but she said, "I'm Becky Anderson." All we can do now is pray," Bill said.

This is a lonely time for Bill and Jamey. I'm sure he'd appreciate hearing from his many fans in mid-Michigan. Write to: Bill Anderson, 4223 Lebanon Road, Hermitage, Tenn. 37076.

I believe my cop friends, now. Sooner or later, a drunken driver will bring sadness to your life, too.

Becky's Better

Several weeks ago, I wrote a column about the terrible brain injuries suffered by Becky Anderson, wife of my friend, Bill Anderson, of the Grand Ole Opry. Becky's car was struck head-on by a vehicle driven by a drunken driver.

I heard the pain in Bill's voice when he called to tell me of the tragedy. I asked Onlooker readers to send Bill and Becky some letters of encouragement. The response was overwhelming.

A few days ago, Bill asked to write a guest Onlooker column. Here's what he wrote:

Dear Jim,

I just wanted to drop you a few lines to update you on Becky's condition and to thank, if I may, the countless hundreds of your readers who took the time to drop her a card or a letter after you mentioned her accident in your column.

I can't tell you how touched both of us were by the thoughtful kindness of so many unseen friends. People said that if we were friends of yours, then we were special to them, and the outpouring of their love was just unbelievable. Becky is still going through the cards and reading every single one.

She was in the hospital for three weeks, the first week unconscious and in intensive care. When I first spoke with her doctors the morning following the accident, they told me she had a fifty-fifty chance of surviving. The first forty-eight hours were the most critical, they said, and since we were dealing primarily with brain damage, the most important thing was to keep the swelling down in that area.

It was the longest two days of my life. We marked the hours one by one as they passed. All we could do was wait. Would she know us when she woke up? Would her speech be impaired? Her memory? There were so many unanswered questions.

There were, however, no unanswered prayers. People from all over the world had by this time heard the news, and I can't tell you how many had lifted up her name in prayer. The minister who married us told me in the beginning that, ''The hands that created her are holding her now.'' They certainly were.

She's now at home recuperating slowly, but gaining a little strength every day. It's going to be slow and long, but the doctors have told us she should recover fully.

I hope neither you nor anybody you know ever has to go through an experience like we've gone through. But if you do, I pray you'll have the support and the love of your friends, as we have had. Thanks for being one of my very special buddies!

Well-rounded Education

The regular schooling of hundreds of thousands of boys was interrupted in classrooms all over the land Wednesday.

But somehow I get the feeling that the girls were being educated. All those boys had browbeaten their teachers into turning on the classroom TV set during the World Series.

One Lansing eight-year-old confessed to his dad after school Wednesday that he had "smuggled" his transistor radio into his third-grade classroom.

"I didn't have to use it much, though," he said, "cause the teacher pulled a surprise."

The boy went on to explain: "Our teacher told us she had a surprise for us if we all got our work done in the morning. Then, she brought a TV set into the room as the game was about to start."

The lad explained the reaction of a girl in the class.

"What's on TV?" the girl asked.

"The World Series, dummy," the boy answered.

"What's a World Series?" the girl asked.

"It's the baseball fall classic," the boy answered intelligently.

"What's that?" the girl asked.

"It's the championship game between the Tigers and Cardinals," the boy said impatiently.

"Who are the Tigers and Cardinals?" the girl asked.

Disgusted, the boy chose to ignore the girl.

The boy later told his dad, "Gee, Dad, that girl is really gonna be in trouble someday when she gets married and has kids and a husband and she don't even know nuthin' about baseball."

It all tickles the Onlooker a little because the boy was my son. And little Stevie is right, too. The time to start educating girls about the wonders of baseball is right down there in the third grade.

One thing is for sure — that girl has a long climb to get back on Steve's list.

Hot Dog Heaven

Perhaps the most amazing baseball statistic I ever heard came from Hal Middlesworth, Detroit Tigers public relations officer, who said they sell an average of two hot dogs for every paid admission to Tiger Stadium. "If we have one million in attendance in a year, we sell two million hot dogs," he said.

I had trouble believing that statistic until last Sunday. I watched with my own eyes as Sam Corey ate nine hot dogs at Tiger Stadium. I have two other witnesses, Dr. F.O. Grounds, veterinarian, and Lee Talboys, musician. Corey is a Holt businessman and Delhi Township trustee.

The amazing part is that Corey didn't miss an inning of the double header. He keeps one eye on the field action and uses the other as a hot-dog-vendor spotter. He puts about a half-pint of mustard on every dog. When he leaves the stadium, he looks as if he had taken a bath in the stuff.

Nolan Ryan threw a blazing fastball, and I said, "Wow! That had a lot of mustard on it." Corey thought I was talking about his hot dog.

Asked how in the world he could eat that many hot dogs, Corey gave the same answer he gives to all questions asked of him in Tiger Stadium: "Sure is great to be down at the old ball park."

Incidentally, nine hot dogs in eighteen innings is not a Corey record. "I don't think Sam was feeling well today," Talboys said. "I've seen him eat nine dogs in a single game."

Doc Grounds watched Corey all afternoon. "It was more exciting than the ballgames," Doc said. "Corey reminds me of a beagle. They'll eat anything from hot dogs to tin foil."

I don't know if Corey's stomach was in distress Monday morning, but there was distress around the Ingham County offices in the former Auto Owners building in downtown Lansing Monday morning. In fact, the county offices were flying the international distress signal. They had the American flag upside down.

For Corey, I'd suggest Alka Seltzer. For the county building janitor, I'd suggest going to bed earlier on Sunday night. You don't suppose he was standing on his head when he put up that flag, do you?

McAuliffe the Fan

Dick McAuliffe, former Detroit Tiger second baseman, answered his phone in Connecticut when I dialed him early in the morning, after the eleventh-inning Tiger win over Kansas City.

"This is a newspaper columnist, and I'd like to do a column on whatever happened to Dick McAuliffe," I said.

"You can't fool me, Jim Hough. I know your voice. Let's get right to it and discuss baseball. Isn't this great? Aren't those Tigers something? Say, Jim, can you get tickets? My son Mike and I want to go to the World Series," Mac said.

"Whoa, Mac," I said. "I have some questions for the Tiger second baseman who starred in the 1968 World Series. You are sounding more like a fan."

"Yeah, I'm a fan. I've always been a fan. I was a fan when I was a player. I suppose you'd like me to compare the 1984 Tigers with the 1968 Tigers," he said.

Yeah.

"This club is better than the '68 team. It has more depth, more speed and a better bullpen. Our '68 team had more power and more offense, but this is a better-balanced team. It has no superstars, just a lot of good players all doing their jobs very well. That's my kind of team.

"Superstars get all the publicity, but it is often the lesser players who make the big play or get the big hit that keeps the club in the race. It was that way in 1968, too. Everyone talks about the stars of that team, but it was the big hits and the big plays of men like Ray Oyler, Tom Matchick and Dick Tracewski that made the season successful. Teamwork, that's what it takes to make a successful baseball team."

Was the 1968 World Series your biggest thrill in baseball?

"Yes, Jim, for sure. But it was not just the thrill of playing in the World Series. It was the special thrill I felt in playing in the World Series in front of Tiger fans. I don't know whether you've thought about it much, but Tiger fans are special. They are mostly of the working class — hard-working people who really know their baseball. And they have that super attitude. I have often seen Tiger fans come to their feet to applaud a great play by an opposing player. It always made me feel great to see that. You don't see that much in other parks around the league.

"My thrill came in seeing how much a World Series meant to those fans. I scored five runs in that World Series, and I feel like I made some good contributions. But none of that thrilled me as much as do-ing it for Tiger fans,'' he said.

Do you have any baseball goals for the future?

"Yes, I want to fly to Detroit and sit there in the stands with those fans. I want to attend the 1984 World Series in Detroit as a fan. It just wouldn't surprise me if that thrill equalled those I had as a player on that field sixteen years ago,'' he said.

There, reader, if you got this far, you now have some idea of why I am so proud to call Dick McAuliffe a friend. We hope to attend this World Series together. This time, we'll both be fans.

Batting Bats

An East Lansing man wanted to build a rose trellis at his home. He went to Capitol City Lumber Company and picked out several narrow, eight-feet-long boards.

As he approached the checkout counter, he heard a scream and saw people ducking under the counters. A bat had entered the room and was flitting and zig-zagging around.

While the lumber company employees hurriedly pondered a course of action to get rid of the bat, the East Lansing man put aside all of his boards except one. He took a step forward, assuming a baseball batting stance, and took a mighty swing at the zig-zagging bat. Whack! He scored a perfect hit. The bat fell dead on the floor.

The East Lansing man then paid for the lumber and walked out of the building. At his departure, there were many comments about his batting skill. "Did you see that? He hit it on the first swing. What an eye," said one of the employees.

Well, the Onlooker has a scoop for Capitol City Lumber's owner, Jim Olson, and his staff. The man who swung that lumber was none other than Danny Litwhiler, longtime major league baseball player and retired MSU baseball coach.

"Awww, it was nothing," said Danny. "It was like hitting a knuckleball. Heck, I've faced major league knuckleballers with pitches that zigged and zagged more than that bat."

Obviously, Danny still has a great eye at the bat. I wonder how many bats he has broken in his life?

Donnie Flies the Coup

"My gosh, I just saw a bird about six feet tall and weighing about eighty pounds."

Comments like that have been heard many times in the past two weeks near Grand Ledge. While most folks suspect those reports are coming from people suffering from hallucinations, one Grand Ledge man had no trouble believing the stories.

Tom McNeil, owner of a Grand Ledge supermarket, knew those people were seeing Donnie, his pet rhea, who escaped from his pen at Mt. Hope and Oneida highways about two weeks ago.

Tom told the Onlooker about Donnie, saying, "I have a little pond at my home, where I keep geese and other wildlife. I bought the rhea, a South American bird now about five feet high and weighing about eighty pounds. I've had him for three years, and he has escaped from the corral two times in the past two months.

"It's a real problem when Donnie is loose. He's harmless, but he is nearly impossible to catch. He can run with great speed, and he can turn on a dime. I have to gather about ten willing and courageous friends to surround him and tackle him. It takes at least one strong man on each of Donnie's legs. We'll have to stage another roundup, I guess."

And where is Donnie now?

"He's just down the road a bit. He is standing most of the time in front of a big picture window and staring in there at his reflection. I think it must be mating time. I can imagine the feeling the people in that house must have had the first time they looked out their window and saw old Donnie peering in at them," he said.

What does Donnie eat?

"Mice, rats, snakes and such. He has to have protein. When he's home, we feed him dog food. He loves dog food, but he hates my dog. It was the dog that chased him out of the pen, I think.

"I hope he gets hungry and comes home, but I doubt it. I figure we'll have to catch him again. He's an old pro now and very wary. This roundup will be difficult, and we have to be so careful to avoid hurting Donnie," Tom said.

It's simple, Tom. Just put a mirror in Donnie's pen, so he can admire himself during mating season. Better yet, get him a girlfriend.

Hidden Gifts

A lump came into my throat as my son Steve called from Denver, Colorado, to say he would not be able to come home for Christmas. There was a lump in his throat, too, I could tell.

He explained that he was on a new job and had no vacation built up. He could only get Christmas Day off.

"I like the job a lot, Dad, and I think I'd lose it if I was absent. It is too expensive to fly home just for a few hours," he said. Steve is nineteen. Holiday times have always been important to him because they meant family togetherness.

I saw a tear as his mother received he news. "It will be our first Christmas without the whole family together," she said.

I felt sorry for myself — until I began to think of some friends of mine and the kind of Christmas grief they must bear today.

There is my pal, Ray Morris. He is still fighting for his life at Ingham Medical Hospital, where he has been a patient since he was struck by a car while jogging five weeks ago. I started to say "Merry Christmas" in a note to Ray. I tore it up. The words seemed empty.

When I talked with Ray's wife Winifred, she said, "Don't worry, Jim, it is a Merry Christmas for us. We're grateful to have Ray alive."

Then I thought about Joyce Chard, widow of Jack Chard. Her home will be empty — her first Christmas without him.

And there is another friend, Joe Farhat. Joe just learned that his kidneys have failed. He just retired, but now he will have to go on the kidney machine. Christmas doesn't seem merry for Joe.

And what about the family of Ken Brecht? Ken, a longtime friend of mine and a veteran State Journal printer, died Friday of a heart attack. He was only thirty-nine.

It was also hard to say "Merry Christmas" to another close friend, Ed Sears. Ed was on the verge of tears. He was in town to visit his brother, Max, who is seriously ill with cancer.

"Merry Christmas" was hard to say to Rose Hudson. She has no family. She is very elderly and attempting to recover from a fractured hip at Burcham Hills Retirement Center's nursing section.

Other friends of ours, struggling with a marital problem, were not saying "Merry Christmas" with much enthusiasm.

Journal reporter John Schneider told me a story that was more than I could take. He told me about a woman who goes every Christmas Eve to the Ingham County Extended Care facility with a poinsettia for her son. He doesn't know she's there. He has been in a coma for five years, ever since he was in an auto crash. She doesn't know what Merry Christmas means anymore.

Just now, my city editor George Pinkerton interrupted me in this writing. I looked into his worried face. We have been friends, and our sons Steve and Tim are buddies.

"Tim's in a South Dakota hospital, Jim. He's in critical condition. He was just in an auto crash on his way home for Christmas. They say he has serious head and back injuries. My wife is on a plane headed out there now," George said. Some Christmas for the Pinkertons, eh?

Steve won't make it home for Christmas. But ours will surely be a Merry Christmas compared to many. It is truly an important time when you suddenly gain perspective — a realization that life is pretty good to you after all.

We'll have a long phone conversation with Steve today. I will appreciate it more, knowing so many families have been cheated of that simple pleasure.

Train Derails Man

Most of you know that Terry Braverman is a powerful figure as director of MSU's Ralph Young Fund — but I'll bet nobody thought he was powerful enough to stop a train.

He did it Friday morning.

Terry's wife Gail was taking the early-morning train from East Lansing to Chicago, to visit her mother-in-law. Terry drove her to the station at Trowbridge Road and helped her aboard.

He went with Gail through several cars to the front of the train and helped her get settled in her seat. They visited a moment and had a good-bye kiss. Terry then began making his way to the rear of the train to depart.

Midway in the trip, the train began to roll, picking up speed rapidly. Terry yelled for a conductor and ran through the aisles pushing people aside in a great panic. He did not want to go to Chicago.

A train official approached him and said, "Hey, mister, you don't belong on this train."

"Who knows that better than me? Man, get this thing stopped," Terry said.

The train official pulled the emergency stop cord. It didn't work — inoperable in that car. They ran to another car and made another try. Finally, the conductor arrived and agreed to stop the train in Lansing at Washington Avenue, near the Depot Restaurant. Terry breathed a sigh of relief.

The train stopped and the conductor quickly put a step down for Terry. Terry started down and saw that he was looking right smack into the Grand River. "Man, this isn't Washington Avenue," he protested.

"Washington Avenue?" the conductor said, "I thought you said to stop at Pennsylvania Avenue."

The conductor started the train again and ordered another stop at Washington Avenue. At Washington the train screeched to a stop again. This time, other train officials arrived at Terry's car, and they all began a big, intense argument with the conductor about why he had been stopping the train so much.

In the middle of their argument, Terry saw his chance. He jumped off. He made his way up the tracks and into the Depot Restaurant where there were a couple of early-morning drinkers at the bar. One of them saw Terry get off the train.

"Gee, Mister, you must be a pretty important dude. The last time the train stopped to let anyone off here it was President Ford."

Terry told them the story of his train adventure. One of the bar patrons laughed so hard he spilled his drink on the floor.

"Don't ask for an explanation, just come to Lansing at the Depot Restaurant and pick me up," Terry said on the phone to someone in his office.

His wife probably wondered why the train was stopping so much. She'll find out when she gets home and reads the Onlooker.

Picture This

Although it is often embarrassing, the story behind the story is often the best story. And the Onlooker just can't resist embarrassing State Journal photographer Dave Webb.

Dave was sent out to take pictures of the Beaumont Tower bells at Michigan State University. He climbed up in the tower and was told by officials there that he could just take his time and get any pictures he wanted.

Dave looked around, climbed up higher on a small ladder, began setting up his lights and soon was about ready to snap a few shots.

Then, he began hearing the clicking and whirring of mechanisms below him. Soon, just as he feared, the worst was about to happen. It was 5:30 p.m., and the bells were about to ring.

And sure enough, BONG, BONG, BONG, and more bongs rang out. Webb said it was like being inside a barrel while somebody clobbered it with a sledge hammer.

"I just hung on for dear life," Dave said.

But the Onlooker happens to know that Webb was glad to get out of there, and that he does not plan to return right away.

Trouble in Paradise

I think I know one young man who is happy summer is over and school is about to begin again. The young man is my son Steve, seventeen, who will begin his senior year at Harry Hill High School.

Steve spent the summer at Paradise, working as a dishwasher. He and his dog spent the summer there at our cabin. He had my old jeep for transportation.

Well, the first thing that happened was that the jeep radiator sprung a big leak, and the repair cost him eight-five dollars. Two weeks later, the jeep water pump broke and that cost him sixty-two dollars. Then the brakes went out. That bill is pending.

I thought our troubles had ended because Steve was due to load his black Labrador, Candy, and his suitcase into the jeep to return home this weekend. Then, the phone rang with another in the long summer series of collect calls to Dad.

"First off, Dad, I want you to know that I have been very, very, very careful in how I've driven the jeep. I have not abused it at all..."

Yeah, Son, what broke now, I asked.

"The oil pump. We need a new oil pump. I think it will cost about forty dollars," he said.

After my groans had ended and the conversation turned to other things, Steve said: "Dad, are you calmed down pretty good now? If so, I have some other bad news for you."

Lay it on me, I said.

"Candy had a fight with a skunk this morning. She smells so bad that I couldn't get near her. I put her on the front porch of the cabin, and I went to work. To be honest, Dad, I don't even want to go back to the cabin. You can't believe how bad she stinks. What do I do now?"

Well, I said, do the windows work OK on the jeep?

"Yes," he answered, "why do you ask that?"

Because you'll have to open them wide as you head home with that dog on Sunday, I said. Give her a bath in tomato juice, and, Son, for Pete's sake, don't call me anymore. I can't take it. Just withdraw your meager summer earnings from the bank and get home as soon as you can — before the Mackinac Bridge falls into the Straits or something.

Working for a Living

Some days Onlooker readers leave me shaking my head in wonder.

One day last week, a woman called to suggest an Onlooker item, saying: "My husband and I met on the thirteenth and were married a few months later on the thirteenth. Our child was born on the thirteenth. My husband and I were separated on the thirteenth, and our divorce was later final on the thirteenth."

I was just getting over that one when a woman called to say: "Now look here, just take this down. I want you to put this in the Onlooker, do you understand? Are you taking this down?"

"Shucks, Ma'am, you haven't said anything yet," I said.

"Well, I'm going to tell you something, and I want you to take it down," she continued. "And another thing, I'm not going to give you my name and address. I don't want you to have my name or address.

"By the way, if you put this in the paper, will you send me a copy?"

And all of you editors think it's easy to be the Onlooker...

House Holds Memories

For many years, it was fun to take my friends by an old, abandoned house in Trout Lake, a tiny town north of St. Ignace along U.S. 123.

"There, you are looking at the birthplace of the Onlooker," I'd say to the bored passengers. "I was born right there in that upstairs bedroom. My dad went rushing out in the dark of the night to find a neighbor woman to help, and he ran nose-to-nose with a horse grazing in that field right there. Dad says he nearly had a heart attack. He's afraid of any animal bigger than a chipmunk..."

Few of the passengers I've hauled by that house over the years en route to our cabin in Paradise have ever been impressed.

The last time I did it was with a gang of my State Journal colleagues. We were riding in a van and headed north on a euchre-playing trip to my cabin. I made my usual tour-guide speech about my birthplace. There was only one response from the back of the van: "Whose deal?" someone asked.

I guess I can understand their indiffference. After all, who cares about such things? But that old house always meant something to me, even though I was a small child when my family moved from there. The house had also been occupied by my grandmother and grandfather. I don't remember my grandfather. I was very young when he died right there in that house, in the arms of his son, my father.

Trout Lake was a great community in those days — a center of railroads and lumber. For the years I grew up around there, Trout Lake was, for me, a metropolis — the only place that had cement sidewalks where a kid could scoot along with one knee in his little red wagon to Mr. Logan's store, where he could buy a sack of candy for a penny.

I used to kid my friends about a groundswell of interest in restoring the old home, or the Michigan Historical Commission making it a historical monument — birthplace of Jim Hough.

Nothing like that can ever happen now.

On a recent trip to the cabin, we drove by the old home. It had been burned down — either by vandals or by a Trout Lake community clean-up committee.

Despite all the joking about that old house over the years, a lump of sadness hit my throat when I saw that pile of charred wreckage. A lot of important family history had gone up in smoke.

Trout Lake can never be the same for me.

Mighty Mouse

Seven-year-old Lynn Tirban, son of Mr. and Mrs. Howard Tirban, didn't make it to school opening day because he had an encounter with a very ferocious mouse.

The mouse bit him, and he had to have a tetanus shot, and the tetanus shot caused a severe reaction, and Lynn's arm was swollen, and...that darned old mouse anyway.

The lad was riding his bike when a cat chased a mouse across the sidewalk. The boy tried to avoid the cat, and his bike swerved. Lynn fell off and the mouse ran at his hand and bit him.

Then the mouse ran out into the street and was struck by a car. The cat then picked up the mouse and started to eat it. Lynn picked up the mouse and took it home. His mother took the mouse to the health department to check it for rabies. The test was negative, but Lynn had to have a tetanus shot.

And, that's the way it goes, sometimes, when you're riding your bike the day before school opens.

*A columnist needs
and welcomes
guest columns.*

*Here are a few of
the Onlooker's favorites.*

Daughterly Duties

by Linda Hough
(The Onlooker's sixteen-year-old daughter)

People often ask me what it's like to be the daughter of the Onlooker.

It's like being a secretary who never gets a paycheck, that's what it's like.

My dad comes home with a hundred letters he got that day in his latest stupid contest and says, "Linda, how about reading these for me, to help me pick a winner?"

Dad, as some readers know, has severe vision problems and can't read without high-powered glasses. That means, I guess, that I'm his secretary. Almost every night we sit down to read his mail and pick out items that he can use in future columns. Now, since Dad is recovering from an operation, I get a chance to write a column of my own.

Sometimes when I read for Dad, I'd rather be out with friends, but it's not so bad because his mail is interesting. Usually the mail is good deeds and such. Maybe that's what makes Dad an optimist.

But there is another side to it all. How do you explain to your high school English teacher why you don't write as well as your dad? And the kidding I get from my friends every time Dad mentions my name in his columns. I have threatened him more than once for that.

He says I get embarrassed too easily. Maybe I do. But when I get introduced at parties and such, people always add, "She's the daughter of the Onlooker." That makes me want to slink off into a corner.

Then there are the people who bring me stuff they want me to give my dad for the column. I learned a long time ago that Dad doesn't like that kind of pressure. He's told me many times, "That's not fair to other readers, Linda. Just tell the people to write me a letter or call me up," he always says.

Then there are the people who talk to me about a certain column Dad wrote. I often have to fake it, because I don't read Dad's column every day.

Dad will have a relapse when he reads that, but it's the truth. I think that is probably true of my brother, too. If he were honest with you, he would admit he doesn't read the column every day. Dad always laughs and says he doesn't read it either. "It's bad enough having to write it," he always says.

Maybe our family doesn't read the Onlooker every day, but we hear about it often. Dad tells us at dinner about things he dealt with that day. He loves it when his column has been able to find a lost Leader Dog, or when he just helped some poor family.

I may not be a regular reader of his column, but I am one of his regular admirers.

Anderson on the Opry

by Bill Anderson
(Country singer)

NASHVILLE, Tenn. — By all rights, Jim Hough and I should trade occupations. I'm in the country music business down here in Nashville, and there's nobody I know in this world who loves country music more than Jim.

He, of course, is a newspaper writer, and hanging just above the big guitar that sits in my Music City office is my diploma from the Henry W. Grandy School of Journalism at the University of Georgia that says I at least completed four years of study to do what Jim does.

He asked me to dust off my Olivetti for this occasion, and I accepted the challenge with glee. May this column, in turn, serve as Jim's personal invitation to come sing on the Grand Ole Opry anytime the spirit moves him. (Jim's recovering from surgery.)

For those of you who don't already know, Jim Hough has appeared on the Opry stage in front of a packed house on a Saturday night in the old Ryman Auditorium. I know, because I'm the one who dragged him out there!

He was a backstage visitor and wanted to get a better view of the proceedings. I told him to come on out and join us. He thought I was kidding and balked at my suggestion, but the Opry is anything but a formal occasion. So, I just grabbed his sleeve, and before he could say "Minnie Pearl," he was standing on the very spot where the greats of country music come to perform.

This may seem insignificant to those of you who prefer your opera to be "Metropolitan," rather than "Grand Ole," but to somebody with pickin' and singin' in his soul, being on stage at the Grand Ole Opry is akin to toeing the rubber at Yankee Stadium, taking the checkered flag at Indianapolis, sinking a hole-in-one at Pebble Beach, or playing a love scene with Sophia Loren. In other words, what else in life is left?

People ask me all the time if the Opry has lost anything in its move from the ancient Ryman to its posh new surroundings at Opryland, U.S.A. "How can the feeling be the same?" they ask. "How can everybody be as 'at home'?"

I must admit that I was concerned when I heard a few years ago that we were to someday have a new home. Luckily, officials of the National Life & Accident Insurance Company, who own radio station WSM and the Grand Ole Opry, worried over it, too.

So much, in fact, that when they were designing the new structure, they locked horns with more than one architect who questioned their reasoning behind the wide aisles in the house ("So the fans can still come down and take pictures of the stars," said WSM.); the concession stands being not in the lobby, but alongside the stage on either end ("So the fans getting a box of popcorn won't miss any of the show," said WSM.); and the hard, church-like pews for seating, rather than plush, theater-style chairs in most modern auditoriums ("Because that's what makes the Opry the Opry," WSM said.).

We all knew the minute the curtain went up on opening night in March, 1974, that WSM had guessed right. The Opry House was loaded to the rafters with dignitaries, fans, the President of the United States, and curiosity seekers.

At precisely 6:30 p.m., the big velvet curtain began to rise, and every member of the Opry cast, totaling some sixty star performers and over one hundred supporting musicians, dancers, background singers, and announcers, strode onto the mammoth stage.

A large movie screen was lowered across the front of the stage, however, and the entertainers were hidden from the view of the audience. A black and white film of the Solemn Ole Judge George D. Hay, the man who gave the Opry its name in 1925, flashed on the screen, and for the first time in nearly twenty years, his voice rang out: "Presenting...the Grand Ole Opry! Let 'er go boys!"

Immediately, a 1941 film clip of a young Roy Acuff came onto the screen and the Smokey Mountain Boys broke into the legendary "Wabash Cannonball."

The film had run for about fifteen seconds when the movie screen began to slowly ascend and a grey-haired, seventy-year-old Acuff led his same Smokey Mountain Boys to the new microphone on the new stage and began singing "Wabash Cannonball" right along with the voice and image on the screen.

The crowd was motionless. You could almost hear the goosebumps breaking out on forty-four hundred sets of arms, and the tears welling up in eighty-eight hundred eyes. Minnie Pearl was standing next to me on the crowded stage, and when the curtain and the movie screen were fully raised, she looked out into the jammed hall and whispered almost to herself, "Stand up, everybody, stand up!"

It was as though they all heard her command. Forty-four hundred people rose as one and gave the Opry and its people and its new home the greatest ovation I have ever heard.

The artists appeared on stage in alphabetical order that night, and Anderson followed Acuff. I walked nervously but proudly to that microphone, muttered something about finally being glad after all these years that my name started with an "A" (It's rough on you when you're in school.) and broke into the song that got me on the the Opry in the first place...a timely little epic called "Po' Folks."

It wasn't until I was well into the song, however, that I glanced down and realized that the circle of stage I was standing on was a darker shade of wood than the rest of the area around it. And then I remembered: They had cut a six-foot circle from the front-center section of the old Ryman stage and brought it to the new Opry House.

And there I was, truly standing on the very spot where Hank Williams had cried the "Lovesick Blues"; where Patsy Cline had sung "I Fall to Pieces"; and where Charlie Pride had told the world, when he became the first black to appear on the modern-day Opry, "I'm glad I'm an American."

Oh, yes...and where Jim Hough had said, "Boy, if the folks back in Lansing could only see me now!"

Milliken on Lansing Bridges

by Gov. William Milliken
(Written in January, 1975)

I recall a humid August morning when Jim Hough and I set a fast pace as we walked to work together. That was the day of the famous "Governor's Logan Street Bridge Walk."

Once we got downtown, Jim complained that he had worked so hard already, he didn't know if he was going to be able to write his column that day. I was tired, too, but my job is easier. And so, in an expansive moment, I said, "Jim, if you end up in the hospital, I'll write your column for you."

Jim is in the hospital, and I'm writing this column.

Talk about holding a politician to his promises.

Talk about delayed reaction. That bridge walk was in 1969.

People are always telling me how to run the state. Now it's my turn. Now that I've got a forum, I'm going to tell the mayor and council how to run this town. (Already I'm learning that it's more fun to be the teller than the tellee.)

On the subject of bridges, and on the subject of running this town, I would like to suggest to the powers that be that they take advantage of this once-in-a-lifetime opportunity to create a beautiful new approach to Lansing's greatest landmark.

The landmark I'm referring to is the State Capitol, of course, and the approach is the Michigan Avenue bridge.

A bridge can be a purely functional thing — or, it can be a beautiful addition to the scene. The bridges of Paris are works of art in themselves. The Mackinac Bridge is a worthy addition to the already-beautiful scenery of the Straits of Mackinac. The Belle Isle Bridge in Detroit is a beautiful thing.

And now that Lansing is opening up its waterfront, we're coming to realize that the Kalamazoo and Shiawassee Street bridges are really rather pleasant to look at. In fact, a picture in a recent edition of the State Journal showed the lights of the Shiawassee Street bridge at night and compared it to a Paris scene.

Now, shouldn't the bridge carrying Lansing's major street across Lansing's major river be a structure that the town can take pride in? I would hope that the bridge now being built will be an attractive structure, a worthy approach to the Capitol.

Picture it: Driving down Michigan Avenue at sundown, with the Capitol dome silhouetted against the sky, framed by two rows of graceful lightposts that line the bridge.

We could make its dedication an early Bicentennial event. We could even name the bridge after some famous local person, like Jim Hough — or some other columnist.

93

Spring Training Awe

by Sam Corey
(Written in March, 1980)

LAKELAND, Fla. — Jim Hough, the columnist, he's the one being paid to fill this space. But Jim is like a kid in a candy shop down here. He is so bedazzled, amazed and agog at the Detroit Tiger's spring training camp that he has forgotten that columnists write columns.

He hasn't given a single thought to the State Journal since we left Lansing last Thursday in a snowstorm. I was afraid he would get fired if he didn't write something, so I sat down at his typewriter.

I'm funnin' you a little, readers. The truth is that I'm the kid in the candy shop. Next to my family, my greatest love is baseball — Tiger baseball. I must look like a country- hick kid looking at tall buildings on his first trip to New York City.

I stand wide-eyed and open-mouthed as I talk face to face with great Tiger personalities — Al Kaline, Sparky Anderson, Gates Brown, Kirk Gibson, Rich Leach, Lance Parrish and others.

I have pretended to be a newspaperman, flashing press credentials, as I enter the locker room or take strolls to the batting cage. I think, however, that they are a little suspicious when I quit interviewing and start asking for autographs. But each young Tiger I've met so far has been a courteous and polite young man, the kind who makes you proud.

My biggest thrill came on the first night in Lakeland. I met Hoot Evers. Can you believe that? Hoot was my biggest baseball hero when I was a kid, back in the days when Jim Hough and I used to skip school and hitchhike to Tiger Stadium.

Today, Hoot is in charge of the Tigers' minor league system. Was I nervous talking to Hoot in person? Not a chance. That's because Hoot Evers is one neat man who quickly puts you at ease. In minutes, we were old friends.

My second biggest thrill came two days later, when I saw Hoot again, and he said, "Hi, Sam. How's it going as a rookie reporter?" Imagine that. Hoot remembered my name.

Meeting three other Detroit Tiger personalities probably gave me thrill number three. They are not players, but are Hall of Famers in the broadcast world — Ernie Harwell, Paul Carey and Joe Gentile. For many years I have loved those voices — Ernie and Paul on the radio broadcasts, and Joe as the stadium announcer.

I sat in the spacious press box during a game at the Boston Red Sox Park in Winterhaven. I felt as though I should have pinched myself to

94

see if it was all a dream. We had just left the field where we had talked with so many great stars. Suddenly a man tapped me on the shoulder from behind. As I turned he said, ''Hi, I'm Ernie Harwell. I don't think we've met.''

How about that, sports fans? There I was, having a face to face talk with the Great Ernie Harwell himself.

What's that? Whatever happened to Jim Hough? Well, the last time I saw him, he was visiting with our next-door neighbor at the hotel, John Hiller. In Jim's mind, John is King Tiger. Maybe Jim can write a column again some day, if he ever gets back down to Earth.

Jim keeps telling me he misses his dog Candy. But what I miss most are my hot dog runners at baseball games, Dr. Jack Grounds, Lee Talboys and Bud Schmidt. Yeah, the mustard and hot dog stock are up, and we're having a great time. I don't know how it could possibly be more fun.

The Big Five-Zero

by Mark Nixon
(Written in March, 1982)

Jim doesn't know about this, and if he did, he would probably give it the Onlooker Ax. Jim likes surprises as much as he likes hockey and the opera, which isn't at all.

But I had the editors' permission to write this surprise Onlooker. More than that, I had their blessing. So, Jim, do what you always do when something goes wrong — blame it on the editors.

You see, today is Jim Hough's fiftieth birthday. It's the same birthday he lamented in an earlier column; the same one he threw a surprise birthday party for. That's right, he hates surprises so much that he scuttled any surprise by throwing a party for himself.

And what a party it was. There was a bagpiper (Jim hates bagpipes.) and a little guy in a tutu (I'm not sure how he stands on tutus.). There was also a special dedication from his good friend, country music star Bill Anderson. The dedication came over Nashville's Grand Ole Opry station, WSM. It was twelve-thirty Sunday morning, and there was Jim with his ear to a portable radio, listening to the song dedicated to him, "Too Old to Cut the Mustard."

But this column isn't to poke fun at Jim's advancing age. This column is about youth.

All of us, at one time or another, goes chasing after the fabled fountain of youth. Some of us — if we get lucky or wise enough — stop looking elsewhere and find that youth lies closer to the heart than the date on a birth certificate. I once knew a man who died young, although he was sixty-seven. I know others under forty who have all but given up on life's promise and are very, very old.

Nobody owns the secret of being young, nor can they pass it on to a friend. But when you meet someone with that secret, you just know it. Meeting Jim for the first time or for the one- thousandth time, you just know it.

Jim's party last Saturday was not to celebrate his fiftieth birthday. It was to celebrate his youth. He is the youngest fifty-year-old I know.

It is no accident that when young reporters begin work at the Lansing State Journal, many are drawn to the desk in the corner of the newsroom where Jim sits. It is no coincidence that some of the younger people in the newsroom suggested a surprise Onlooker column to honor him today.

And, it is no accident that many of his faithful readers are of retirement age. They find in his column a youthful vigor that seems to shout, "Hey, world! I'm alive and kicking!" They find, perhaps, a promise of a better day; not tomorrow, but right now, today.

Sounds like I'm putting the guy on a pedestal, right?

Right. But you should know that Jim never wanted a pedestal higher than a soapbox, where he could stand and say something encouraging about his fellow man or maybe needle us about our follies. That's not such a terrible pedestal to endure, is it?

There were tons of people at Jim's surprise party Saturday. A lot of people hugged him, because they truly love the man. There was also, maybe, the unconscious wish that some of his youthfulness would rub off.

Too old to cut the mustard? How are you going to convince a kid from the U.P. of that?

Insightful Onlooker

by Neil Hunter

With the master scribe of this column away on vacation for a week, it has been asked of the lesser talent around the State Journal editorial department to fill this space with contributions that might pass as somewhere near equal to the regular fare.

The real Jim Hough is up in Canada, wetting a trout line at some remote lake, along with a troupe of his fun-loving fishing buddies, who make this venture a kind of annual experience in outdoor camaraderie.

Good fellowship between humans is Jim's long suit, be it in the office or out under the pines.

To his readers, who know Jim only through the printed word, this might be a good time to say that he is a rare person to know — the kind you are most fortunate to have as a friend during life's short trip in time. For Jim fits Kipling's description of the utopian person (in his poem "If"), who can walk with kings, but keep the common touch.

You can read columns of fine prose in newspapers across the breadth of the land. But there are few with the depth of understanding that is sprinkled through Jim's Onlooker. This we believe, and this we've heard so often from others.

Maybe that is because the Onlooker column — by its regular author — is written on a typewriter with much larger than regular-size print.

The size of the type is of no matter, but the fact that it is so large might tip you off to the fact that Jim tackles his job with a severe visual handicap.

But, like other people with handicaps, your Onlooker is almost without peer in his attitude of braveness which, coupled with his depth of human understanding, brings sunshine into this space.

When Jim's back, and if he happens to read this, mark it down, he'll come out with his usual, "Oh, hawgh wash. Whadja' say that for? There are lots of others in worse predicaments."

Looking for Thoreau

by John Ward
(Written on January 1, 1969)

What makes the Onlooker tick?

Few of his thousands of readers have had the opportunity to meet him. One new addition to the State Journal staff said he had imagined the Onlooker to be a little, old sage man.

Jim Hough, the Onlooker, is not little, nor is he old, and some might say he isn't sage, for he is spending this week of his vacation on Lake Superior with his wife and children.

When hundreds of others are looking forward to a week in warm Florida, why would a man wish to drive above the Straits to a little town called Paradise, park his car and snowshoe several miles to a little cabin erected on a beach in front of Lake Superior? There, without telephone, radio, television and many of the "necessities" of everyday life, they are spending this week.

Some would question why this man would want to impose these "hardships" on his family. But we suspect our Onlooker has some of Henry David Thoreau in his blood. He was born and raised in that part of Michigan. He grew up not knowing the wonderful advantages of indoor plumbing and of many other luxuries that are now commonplace.

We suspect that today, while many of us are nursing a headache and sitting in front of the boob tube watching eight hours or so of bowl games and eating the traditional sauerkraut, the Onlooker will be seated by his wood stove in front of his picture window, looking out at his beautiful Lake Superior.

And he will be enjoying what he calls a family affair — an opportunity to get to know his children better, without the interruptions of the telephone and neighborhood children.

In his twenty-four by twenty-four-foot cabin, he will find that peace of heart and mind that passes by so many of us. In the everyday hustle to make a living, we refuse to take time to get away and reflect upon the world about us.

This year there is ample to reflect upon.

Sage? Yes, for he is taking an opportunity to reflect in solitude, to give his family experiences that will be remembered all their lives. A chance to better know himself and his family. This is Jim Hough, the Onlooker.

Happy New Year, Jim.

99